*"Heaven and Earth never agreed better
to frame a place for man's habitation."*

—Captain John Smith

Chesapeake

EXPLORING THE WATER TRAIL
OF CAPTAIN JOHN SMITH

JOHN PAGE WILLIAMS
NATURALIST
CHESAPEAKE BAY FOUNDATION

FOREWORD BY GILBERT M. GROSVENOR

NATIONAL GEOGRAPHIC
WASHINGTON, D.C.

PENNSYLVANIA

SUSQUEHANNOCK

Susquehanna

NEW
JERSEY

Delaware

0 mi   20
0 km   20

North East
Creek

North East
River

Havre de
Grace

Elkton

Elk

Bush

Bohemia

Sassafras

Gunpowder

Baltimore

Chester

Dover

Patapsco
River

Annapolis

VIRGINIA

Arlington
Washington, D.C.
Alexandria   Nacotchtanck
ANACOSTAN
MATTAPANIENT
MARYLAND

Easton

DELAWARE

Moyaons
PISCATAWAY
PATUXENT

Cambridge

CHOPTANK

Choptank

Nanticoke

MATTAWOMAN

Potomac

NANJEMOY
Patawomeck

Cecomocomoco

Patuxent

Chesapeake

NANTICOKE

Salisbury

Wicomico

MATCHOTIC

Bloodsworth
Island

POCOMOKE

Pocomoke

RAPPA-
HANNOCK

Rappahannock

Toppahanock

MD.
VA.

Smith
Island

MATTAPANIENT

Moraughtacund

Bay

POWHATAN

YOUGHTANUND

Mattaponi

Tangier
Island

Pamunkey

Piankatank

The Falls   Richmond
Orapaks
Smith captured
near here

Powhatan

Chickahominy

PAMUNKEY

York

Smith released
Werowocomoco

ACCOMAC

ATLANTIC
OCEAN

CHICKAHOMINY

James

Cape
Charles

Jamestown
Origin of
voyages

Hampton   Kecoughtan

Barge dis-
embarks
from ship
Phoenix

Point Comfort
Cape
Henry

Nansemond
River

Norfolk
CHESAPEAKE

Portsmouth

Capt. John Smith's routes
—— December 1607–January 1608
—— June 2–July 21, 1608
—— July 24–September 7, 1608
✕ Farthest point explored
● Indian chief's town
● Indian village
PAMUNKEY Indian tribe
• Present-day town
▨ Present-day wetland
Present-day shorelines shown

Contents

PRECEDING PAGES: *Sunrise heralds a new day for the creatures living around a tidal creek on the Chesapeake's Eastern Shore.*
MAP: *Captain John Smith was the first Englishman to explore and map the Chesapeake Bay. The routes of his two main voyages are noted here.*

Each year in late fall, tundra swans migrate from the Arctic coast of Alaska and Canada to Chesapeake marshes like this one at the Eastern Shore's Blackwater National Wildlife Refuge near Cambridge, Maryland, to spend the winter.

Foreword

*I*was lucky to grow up fishing, swimming, crabbing, and
boating on the Chesapeake Bay, one of America's crown-jewel
waterways. The bay I remember from my childhood years
teemed with life: fish, crabs, waterfowl, and what we know
today as habitat—vast meadows of underwater grass and
abundant oyster reefs. Exploring the Chesapeake then sparked
my lifelong fascination with discovering the wonders of our
planet. Unfortunately, in recent years, I have seen the health of
the Chesapeake decline under the pressures of its growing
human population.

Thus when my good friend, Pat Noonan, a distinguished
member of National Geographic's Board of Trustees and chairman emeritus of The Conservation Fund, came to me with the
idea to create the Captain John Smith Water Trail to encourage
modern-day Chesapeake explorers, I immediately joined with
him and Will Baker, president of the Chesapeake Bay Foundation, as founding members of the Friends of the Captain John
Smith Chesapeake National Historic Water Trail. Our mission
is to celebrate the unique history and environment of the
Chesapeake Bay while highlighting current efforts to restore
the Chesapeake's health and create a lasting legacy for future
generations. We hope that the water trail will also stimulate
economic development that is compatible with the Chesapeake
ecosystem, especially in the form of heritage tourism. It is

important that the trail attract people—from both near and far—who want to understand how Captain Smith helped shape the colony that gave rise to our country, and the natural ecosystem that allowed it to flourish.

As a complement to the water trail initiative, National Geographic has matched a $1,000,000 contribution from the Lenfest Foundation, establishing a $2,000,000 permanent Chesapeake Bay Geography Education Fund to encourage and support geography and environmental education pertaining to the Chesapeake Bay among K-12 students and teachers residing in the several states within that watershed.

Through a generous contribution from DuPont, National Geographic Maps has produced 100,000 large-format maps of the bay and distributed them free to educators across the bay watershed. One side depicts the bay in Captain John Smith's time, including the natural habitats of the Chesapeake in the early 17th century, the Native American communities, and the routes of Smith's explorations in 1607-09. The other side focuses on the environmental health of the bay today. By comparing the two sides, students, teachers, and the general public will realize how rich Smith's bay was and join efforts to help restore its health.

Through another generous contribution, from Lockheed Martin, National Geographic has created an engaging, innovative, and multifaceted interactive website, Chesapeake: Then and Now (*www.nationalgeographic.com/resources/ngo/education/chesapeake*). It features historical and contemporary stories about the bay and includes an online interactive map that serves students, educators, and the general public.

In this fascinating book, John Page Williams, the long-time senior naturalist at the Chesapeake Bay Foundation, strikes a delightful balance between the history and the natural history of Smith's historic voyages.

Through his own explorations of the bay and its tributaries, he artfully weaves together rich strands of ecological description, historical narrative, and practical information for modern voyagers. Together with the breathtaking, contemporary yet timeless photography of Anthony E. Cook, David Harp, and Bill Portlock (another longtime CBF naturalist), this book recaptures the enduring spirit of the Chesapeake as Smith and the native tribes he met would have known it.

I hope you enjoy Williams's journey in the wake of Captain John Smith. As we approach the 400th anniversary of the founding of the Jamestown settlement, this book serves as a vivid reminder of how much the past—the early ambitions, ideals, Native American culture, and conflicts in the European settlement of North America—abides with us today.

Special thanks to The Conservation Fund and the Chesapeake Bay Foundation along with many public agencies, corporations, nonprofit organizations, and citizens who have been stalwart supporters in this endeavor.

Join us on our website as well and please help us save America's national treasure, the Chesapeake Bay, so future explorers will have the same opportunities to swim, fish, crab, boat, and enjoy a healthy and robust environment.

—GILBERT M. GROSVENOR

Chapter One

*There is but one entraunce by sea into this country,
and that is at the mouth of a very goodly Bay....
Within is a country that may have the prerogative
over the most pleasant places of Europe, Asia,
Africa, or America, for large and pleasant
navigable rivers.... Here are mountains, hils,
plaines, valleys, rivers, and brookes all running
most pleasantly into a faire Bay compassed but for
the mouth with fruitful and delightsome land.*

— Captain John Smith,
Description of Virginia, 1612

World's End Creek on Maryland's Eastern Shore is typical of the tidal tributaries that Captain John Smith and his crews saw during their explorations in the summer of 1608.

PRECEDING PAGES: *A bald cypress tree emerges from the morning mist on the Pocomoke River near Snow Hill, Maryland.*

"A Very Goodly Bay"

The Captain John Smith Water Trail provides a route that boaters can follow to explore the Chesapeake Bay and its tributaries in the wake of Captain John Smith's voyages of 1607-09, while he was a leader in the Jamestown Colony of Virginia. Smith's explorations led to his map of 1612, which provided the first blueprint for European settlement of the Chesapeake region, deeply influencing the history of the 17th century and laying the foundation for American history in succeeding centuries, right up to the present.

Under orders from the Virginia Company of London, sponsor of the Jamestown Colony, Smith's aims in exploring the Chesapeake were to assess the value of its natural resources, including timber, minerals, and furs; the size, distribution, strength, and wealth of the native population; and the potential for trading with them for furs and food. He also sought the fabled but mythical Northwest Passage through the North American continent to the Pacific. Thus his travels took him up most of the rivers to their heads of navigation, especially on the bay's western shore.

The upcoming 400th anniversaries of the founding of Jamestown and of Smith's explorations give modern boaters the opportunity to retrace those voyages of discovery, to feel the excitement of exploration for themselves, and to rediscover the riches of the Chesapeake Bay system, this national treasure in our midst. They also provide an important opportunity to reflect on the nature of the rich Chesapeake ecosystem that Smith and his crews saw, on how profoundly we have changed and unbalanced it in the intervening four centuries, and on what we must do to restore its health.

The 1,700-mile Captain John Smith Water Trail is a composite of Smith's two voyages of exploration up the bay in the summer of 1608

POWHATAN
Held this state & fashion when Capt. Smith
was deliuered to him prisoner
1607

MONACANS

MO NACANS

MANN AH

POWHATAN

P O W H A T A T

MAN-
GOAGS

CHL-
WONS

Iames
towne

Powhatan flu:

poynt comfort

Cape Henry

Cape Charle

Smyths Iles

CHE:

SA:

PEA

KVSKARA

THE

VIRGINIAN SEA

Scale of L

14

RGINIA

Maſſaw- Maſſawomeck omecks

Signification of theſe mark
To the croſſes hath bin diſco
what beyond is by relation
Kings howſes 2
Ordinary howſes 2

HONI SOIT QVI MALY PENSE

ACKS

Manſinitania

ent

Demoterites trees

Quarrengaioack

Buriaus Mount

N

Pamacocack

Tauxcenent

Pamacocack

Cinquaateck

Moyaens

Namaſſinghent

Aſſaomeck

Teſſamatuck

Namoſcraughquend

Wiſſamen

Naxetchtanck

City mount

Quactataugh

chiſes Taquernum Creaſide.

K BAY

Cepowig

The Saſqueſahanougs
are a Gyant like peo= ple &
Otchewig thus a= tyred

Attaock

Teſinah

S A S Q V E
S
H A N
O
V G H

Winstons Iles

Brookes Forest

Ozinies

Point Peſame

Powels Iles

Barnes point

Smiths Iles

Teckrook flu.

Salmitohanough flu.

Saſquehanough

Gunters Harbour

TOCK

WOGHS

Percorens mount

ATOV

WAL KS

A K A C

Aequamachuke

and halfe

Leagues

Chickaholan

Macock

HVKES

5   10   15

red and Diſcribed by Captayne Iohn Smith 1606
Grauen by Wilham Hole

and his other travels on the James, Chickahominy, York, Pamunkey, and Mattaponi Rivers. It builds on and ties together a number of excellent water trails developed by federal, state, and local government agencies and private organizations. Stops along it also take advantage of first-rate facilities that offer visitors insight to Captain John Smith, the Chesapeake he knew, intervening history, and the present day. Many of them belong to the National Park Service Chesapeake Gateways Network and have developed special exhibits to commemorate Captain Smith's explorations. This National Geographic Society Special Publication offers practical considerations and specific information on trail sections for modern-day boaters who wish to follow in Captain Smith's wake.

THE HISTORICAL SIGNIFICANCE OF SMITH'S VOYAGES

*T*he establishment of the Jamestown Colony in Virginia was a product of the age of exploration that began with Columbus in 1492 and continued for the next two and a half centuries. Driven by Spain's discovery of silver and gold in Central and South America, England grew eager to claim riches of its own in the New World, as well as control of a quick route to Asia.

The attempt to colonize the Atlantic coast north of the Spanish colonies in Florida began during the reign of Elizabeth I, the Virgin Queen, in whose honor Sir Walter Raleigh named the territory Virginia. In the 1570s, the Spanish had entered the bay several times and named it the Bay of Santa Maria. Raleigh's first colonists landed just to the south in 1585, in what is now eastern North Carolina. That colony failed, but not before its leader sailed up into the broad mouth of the Chesapeake, came into today's Lynnhaven River, encountered a tribe of Indians who called themselves "Chespioc," and sent word back to London of their discovery.

Elizabeth I died in 1603 and her nephew, James I, ascended to England's throne. In 1605-06, the Virginia Company organized an expedition of three ships, the *Susan Constant, Godspeed,* and *Discovery,* carrying 140 men, including Captain John Smith, to explore the territory inside this Bay of Chespioc, establish a colony, and formally claim the region for England.

After a five-month voyage to Virginia via the West Indies, the three ships landed first on the beach just inside the bay's mouth, near today's Lynnhaven Inlet, on April 26, 1607. There the colonists erected a great cross to claim the land and named the point at the south side of the bay's mouth Cape Henry in honor of the king's son.

They brought out "an open barge of near three tons burthen" that had been built in two halves in England and stored in the hold of one of the ships. It would serve as a tender for the colony. They assembled it on the beach at Cape Henry and commissioned it. This boat was a nameless workhorse, taken for granted and used hard until it disappeared without historical comment as the years wore on. As far as we can tell, it was double-ended, full in the bow and stern, about 30 feet long, with a single mast, two sails, and two banks of oars. In spite of its anonymity, it would play a key role in the development of the colony and the settlement of the Chesapeake region. For the purposes of this narrative, we'll call it the *Discovery Barge*.

At the time, Captain Smith was "restrained as a prisoner," probably aboard the *Susan Constant,* having been there since several noblemen of the expedition accused him of plotting insurrection (a trumped-up charge intended to suppress the outspoken commoner, even if he did know more than they about leadership and survival under difficult conditions).

DISCOVERY BARGE

As we prepare this book for publication, a few boaters on the Chesapeake have already covered much of the Captain John Smith Water Trail. Their vessels range from kayaks and open outboard skiffs to a 22-foot power cruiser and a 34-foot sloop.

The first to cover the trail in one voyage, however, will do so in tribute to Captain Smith's *Discovery Barge*. The new *Discovery Barge,* whose two halves are named *Maryland* (stern) and *Virginia* (bow), was built of lumber from indigenous trees (especially white oak and osage orange) with 17th-century tools and techniques by a crew of professional and volunteer shipwrights at Sultana Shipyard in Chestertown, Maryland, a facility of Sultana Projects, Inc.

The Sultana Projects vessel belongs to a class called the shallop. It is 28 feet 7 inches long, 7 feet 8 inches of beam, with a draft of less than 3 feet, carrying a pair of leeboards in lieu of a centerboard. Propulsion is supplied by six "single-bank" oarsmen, three on each side pulling 14-foot oars, when necessary, plus a foresail and a sprit-rigged main flying from a single mast when possible. It represents the typical utility vessels and workboats of early 17th-century England.

In the summer of 2007, Sultana Projects will engage two paid crews and some volunteers for this barge's voyage around the water trail to commemorate Smith's explorations of 1607-09. A modern outboard chase boat will accompany the barge to deliver supplies, assist with media coverage, and respond to emergencies, if necessary. The barge, however, will rely solely on sail and oar power.

Multiple stops along the water trail will allow the public to visit the vessel and its crew. Several of the stops will include modern reenactments of parts of the original *Discovery Barge*'s voyages, including the First Landing at Cape Henry, Virginia, on April 26, 1607, and the captain's parley with the Susquehannock chiefs on Maryland's Garrett Island on July 21.

With its framing complete, Sultana Projects' Discovery Barge *replica takes shape in the shipyard at Chestertown, Maryland. The barge and its crew will retrace Smith's explorations of the Chesapeake as part of the 400th anniversary of Jamestown's founding.* DETAIL: *The only surviving image of the colony's barge, from Smith's 1612 map.*

Smith was born the son of a yeoman in Lincolnshire in 1580. His father apprenticed him to a nearby merchant while he was in his teens, but that job didn't last long. He volunteered as a soldier of fortune to fight in the Netherlands, France, Hungary (where he earned the battlefield—not nautical—rank of captain), Transylvania (today's Romania), and Morocco. He also endured time as a prisoner of war and a slave in Turkey and Russia. Between adventures, he spent serious time reading and thinking. He was evidently a bright student of human nature as well as a competent soldier. By his mid-20s, he was back in London, where he hired on with the Virginia Company.

Intelligent and energetic, possessed of well-honed common sense and a powerful drive to survive, Smith did not suffer fools gladly, especially those "gentlemen" who thought themselves high-born enough to be his superiors. He clashed repeatedly with such men as he strove to help the colony survive and to carry out the instructions of the Virginia Company to assess the potential riches of the Chesapeake.

He remained on the ship that day when the colony's presumed leaders went ashore in the *Discovery Barge* to explore, though he watched much of what happened, especially a stealthy attack at dusk by five local natives (probably members of the Chespioc tribe). Two of the landing party were injured by the attackers' arrows but recovered.

The day after what we now call the First Landing, Captain Christopher Newport and other presumed leaders opened their orders from the Virginia Company, which had till then been sealed. They included designation of the Governing Council, which to everyone's surprise included Smith. They thus released him, though the other council members voted not to admit him.

After the First Landing, the colonists sailed across the huge river mouth that we know now as Hampton Roads and received a much happier welcome from the Kecoughtan people who lived on the north side, on the site of today's downtown Hampton. They named the point there Comfort because they found not only friendly natives but also a deep channel heading upriver. They would also soon learn from the Kecoughtan the wealth of oysters and fish there, especially around Hampton Bar, in the bight between Hampton and Newport News.

The three ships then began working their way up what the Kecoughtan called the Powhatan River, after the name of the region's paramount chief, but which the English named for King James. One of them probably took the *Discovery Barge* in tow. "Working" is the operative word here. A glance at a map of the lower James reveals the reason: The tidal section of the river winds through more than a dozen large, meandering curves. Seventeenth-century ships did not sail well into the wind, and the meanders guaranteed that they would face headwinds at least part of the way.

According to their instructions from the Virginia Company, the colonists sought a place to settle up the river, to avoid advertising their presence to possible Spanish explorers. They also sought an uninhabited spot where there was deep water close to the bank for landing the ships, and where there was a source of potable fresh water. They made their way—slowly—to the mouth of the Appomattox River, where the present city of Hopewell stands, taking note of possible sites.

Meanwhile, native runners along the trails on both sides of the river sent word of the ships, even as far as the Rappahannock River, 30 miles to the north, where people still sought vengeance for one of their chiefs murdered some years earlier by Europeans (probably

Lilies, opposite, grow in a coastal meadow on Jamestown Island in Colonial National Historical Park in Virginia. If they had the presence of mind to look, the English colonists would have seen ancestors of these lilies when they settled on the island in May 1607.

Natives fishing with spears and nets—"Their manner of fishynge in Virginia" from "A Briefe and True Report of the New Found Land of Virginia," Theodor de Bry (ed.), 1528-1598.

Spanish). The Paspahegh, on the north side of the James, just above the mouth of the Chickahominy, and the Quiyoughcohannock, in the vicinity of today's Claremont, both paddled out to the ships, looking for the attacker, but no Englishman resembled him, and the ships made their way unimpeded.

On May 14, the colonists settled on an island on the north side just below the Chickahominy, primarily because they could bring the ships right in to the bank to unload them. They disembarked, claimed the land, and named it "Jamestowne" in honor of the king. Then "falleth every man to work," according to John Smith's *General History*. The no-nonsense captain undoubtedly did his share and more. The rest, as they say, is history. The development of the Virginia Colony is well documented elsewhere. (See "Further Reading" for useful sources.)

Jamestown's ships proved valuable for navigating the lower sections of the Chesapeake's rivers and carrying heavy loads, but the best all-around vessel turned out to be the *Discovery Barge*. Its first assignment, on which John Smith shipped, was up the James River to its head of navigation, the rocky fall line where it meets sea level at the current site of the City of Richmond.

After that initial voyage, survival preoccupied the minds of the colonists, who found themselves besieged by hunger, brackish drinking water, drought, sometimes-hostile natives, diseases, heat, mosquitoes, and internal squabbles. Smith, however, took seriously the order to explore and made extensive use of the *Discovery Barge*. During the time he spent in Virginia, from the late spring of 1607 to the fall of 1609, he and his crews covered more than 3,000 miles in it, including two trips to the upper Chesapeake in the summer of 1608.

Where did he go? It's easier to say where he didn't. During those voyages, he covered all of the major rivers up to their heads of navigation, with the exceptions of the Eastern Shore's Choptank River, Eastern Bay/Miles River/Wye River complex, and Chester River, and several of the short upper western shore rivers. Using a compass, he took meticulous mapping notes, which he managed to protect from the squalls of wind and rain that the Chesapeake periodically threw at him. Though he and his crewmen wrote several narrative reports on the voyages, Smith often "told his story through his map more than his words," according to *Jamestown Narratives* editor and Smith scholar Edward Wright Haile.

John Smith did not find the quick riches the stockholders of the Virginia Company had hoped for, and even expected. Instead, he gradually developed a sense of the potential of the Chesapeake for English settlers willing to adapt to the specific opportunities the bay offered and work hard to realize them. Just as it had for centuries for the natives, the Chesapeake's sprawling network of navigable rivers became instant infrastructure in a land without roads for those who quickly followed Smith. Using the rivers as highways over the next 70 years, they developed a decentralized economy based on cutting timber and raising tobacco for export, while the waters provided rich harvests of fish and shellfish to sustain their plantations.

In summer, stinging nettles (jellyfish) of the species Chrysaora quinquecirrha *are the bane of Chesapeake swimmers. These planktonic (drifting) cousins of coral feed on tiny fish and crustaceans, disabling them with stinging cells in their tentacles. Most humans who brush against nettles in the water experience a temporary but painful rash.*

The Chesapeake Context

*T*he Chesapeake Bay is the valley of the lower Susquehanna River, an estuary "drowned" by the Atlantic over the past 15,000 years as the ocean rose more than 300 feet during the gradual end of the last ice age.

This view of the Susquehanna, opposite, looks upstream toward Pennsylvania from the northeast corner of Garrett Island. John Smith and his crew would have seen a similar view when they visited the island in 1608 to meet with the Susquehannock chiefs who had paddled down from their town at the site of today's Washingtonboro, Pennsylvania.

The bay reached the basic shape we know today about 3,000 years ago, though it continues to change as sea level rises and some parts of the land sink. The same process flooded the mouths of the other East Coast rivers, from Florida's St. Johns and Georgia's Altamaha to the Delaware, the Hudson, and the Connecticut. On the Chesapeake, it created a shallow tidal settling basin for all the rivers in the system, with an average depth of only 21 feet.

What is unusual about the Susquehanna system is that it has many significant tributaries in its lower section, including the Potomac and the James, which are major rivers in their own right. Over the past 20 years, geologists have uncovered increasing evidence that this gathering of large rivers is at least partially the result of a two-mile-wide meteorite that crashed into Earth approximately at the location of today's Eastern Shore town of Cape Charles. The resulting sinkhole had many ecological consequences, but one of the most important was the capture of those lower tributaries by the Susquehanna.

In terms of watershed acreage (about 64,000 square miles) and average freshwater flow, the whole system is about four times larger than the next largest river on the coast, the Connecticut (the Hudson is close behind the Connecticut). The Susquehanna contributes about half of that flow, the Potomac about 18 percent, the James about 12 percent, and all the others combined, the remaining 20 percent.

When they first entered it in 1607, the Jamestown colonists named the bay "Chesapeake" after the Indian tribe they found living around Cape Henry. A year later, Smith named the largest river at the head of the bay "Sasquesahanough" after the Susquehannock Indians who lived in its valley. The bay and the river are, however, really two sides of the same coin, just as much as the 100-mile tidal river below Washington's Kennedy Center is still the Potomac. If you want a quick estimate of how large the Susquehanna is, compare the upper Chesapeake with the tidal Potomac, and remember that the Potomac in its own right is the eighth largest Atlantic coast river. The Chesapeake is the tidal Susquehanna.

PHYSICS: A RESERVOIR WITHOUT A DAM

*S*alt water is denser than fresh water—the saltier the denser, in fact. Because the bottom of the bay and the tidal portions of the rivers are below sea level, seawater flows in to fill them. Fresh water flowing

In the calm after a Tangier Sound thunder squall blew out the Discovery Barge's *sails, Smith and his crew would have seen ancestors of these black skimmers fishing in the marsh coves of the Limbo Iles (today's Bloodsworth Island). In their concern to make repairs, however, the men may not have noticed these graceful birds.*

down the rivers dilutes it. The denser salty water, though, tends to stay under the fresher surface water.

It's a simple story so far, but it becomes more complicated by variations in rainfall, winds, water temperature, the phases of the moon, and even the Coriolis forces caused by Earth's rotation. Wind is a particularly important factor because so much of the bay is shallow. The physical oceanographers who work on the Chesapeake use advanced math to describe the details, but here are some basics for us lay people:

- The farther down the bay you go, the saltier the water is.
- In a wet year, the main stem of the Chesapeake will be fresh, or nearly so, all the way down to Annapolis. In a dry year, lower bay salinities will be close to seawater, and salt will extend well above Baltimore.
- Most of the time, in any given spot, the salinity at the surface is lower than at the bottom.
- In general, at any given latitude, the water will be saltier on

the eastern side of the bay than on the western side, because of the Coriolis forces.

- Windy weather patterns in spring and fall tend to mix fresher upper layers with salty lower layers; more stable patterns in summer and fall allow the system to stratify.

The surface layers of fresher water sweep some salt down the bay with them, causing salty water to flow in along the bottom to replace it. The result is that there is a net movement of water down the bay at the surface, and a net movement up close to the bottom.

The widening out of the basin into which the Chesapeake's rivers flow and the fact that the tides push upstream twice a day means that net flow slows way down, from a couple of miles per hour to less than a mile per day (tidal currents may move at a couple of knots, but they work both ways). Much of what they bring settles out.

Four hundred years ago, the human population of the Chesapeake watershed was about 100,000 natives with minimal access to metal tools and no domesticated animals larger than dogs. Except for small fields cleared for growing corn, squash, and beans, the land was deeply wooded with virgin forests. The deep, spongy woodland soils soaked up rainwater, filtered it, and released it slowly into brooks, streams, creeks, rivers, and ultimately a bay that was much clearer than it is today.

That runoff carried modest levels of detritus, a "vegetable soup" of decayed plant material and bacteria, and nitrogen and phosphorus, which scientists refer to as "nutrients" because they fertilize the growth

Saltmarsh periwinkles, below, scrape algae off the muddy surfaces of their home marshes when the tide is out. When the tide begins to come back in, they continue feeding by moving up the sturdy stalks of saltmarsh cordgrass.

FOLLOWING PAGES: At sunrise, a great blue heron prepares to fish for breakfast along the shores of the Rappahannock's Cat Point Creek, near Warsaw, Virginia. The land in the background looks much as it did in Smith's time. It is now part of the Rappahannock River Valley National Wildlife Refuge.

A gray fox pup studies its world. Although it will feed primarily on rodents and birds later in life, at this age it is concentrating on insects.

OPPOSITE PAGE:
Fishers are members of the weasel family, kin to river otters and mink. In Smith's time, they lived along the upper bay, its tidal fresh rivers, and the Susquehanna before nearly dying out from heavy trapping. Today, because they are protected and their numbers rising, they are symbols of the value of conservation.

of aquatic plants such as underwater grasses and algae (microscopic plants that drift free or attach to solid surfaces). The grasses in both freshwater and saltwater marshes also soaked up nitrogen and phosphorus, growing lush to offer even more habitat for bay creatures. Because the Chesapeake is such a shallow ecosystem ("The bottom is very close to the top," says noted environmental writer Tom Horton), both groups of plants grew well, furnishing food and habitat for a wide variety of animals, from tiny shrimplike crustaceans to large fish such as sturgeon and striped bass (known universally on the Chesapeake as "rockfish").

From the end of the last ice age until 1607, the bay ecosystem had time to adjust itself to the flow of nitrogen and phosphorus coming down the rivers. The result was a diverse food web that made the most efficient use of available nutrients. Herbivores, carnivores, and omnivores had many choices of food, so that if one source declined temporarily, there were still plenty of alternatives. The harvest technologies available to the Indians limited them to shallow water, so they fitted into the system simply as another group of high-level predators, but they couldn't catch enough to unbalance any of their prey populations.

Meanwhile, populations of fish and shellfish developed natural age distributions in which a number of individuals escaped harvest long enough to die at their species' maximum ages—for example, about 30 years for a rockfish and 15 for an oyster. The latter, in fact, were so abundant that their reefs broke the surface, posing hazards to navigation. Indians harvested them by paddling out, pulling their canoes up onto the reefs, and picking them up. Atlantic sturgeon, which are just reaching maturity when rockfish die of old age, were numerous enough that at certain times of the year, the natives corralled them in the shallows, lassoed their tails, and wrestled them to shore. Meanwhile, the vast meadows of underwater grasses and the marshes attracted wintertime flocks of migratory waterfowl—ducks, geese, and swans—huge enough to "darken the skies."

With their limited technology and tools, the Indians seem primitive to us today, and indeed the Jamestown colonists considered them ignorant, rude savages. In doing so, however, the English displayed their own ignorance. The natives were, in fact, exquisitely attuned to their Chesapeake world. From the Chickahominy River up the bay to the Eastern Shore's Nanticoke and Sassafras, they knew which tidal freshwater marshes grew the best wild rice and arrowhead for starchy food; when the shad, herring, rockfish, and sturgeon made their spawning runs;

and where the best-tasting waterfowl spent the winters. Part of the problem for the first several years of the Jamestown colony stemmed from the disdain of the English for the Indians and their refusal to stoop to learning from them how to feed themselves off the riches of their surroundings. Those "rude salvages" knew well just how rich the Chesapeake Bay ecosystem was in the early 17th century.

"The manner of makinge their boates," opposite, from "A Briefe and True Report of the New Found Land of Virginia," Theodor de Bry *(ed.), 1528-1598. The Algonquian-speaking natives of the Chesapeake region built their canoes by hollowing out large cypress and Atlantic white cedar logs with fire and scrapers made of shells.*

EXPLORATION, 17TH-CENTURY STYLE

*B*y today's standards, the English and Indian vessels of 1607–09 were heavy and clumsy, but they represented the state of boatbuilding art for the time, and people made do with them. Smith's *Discovery Barge* was likely built of oak, with an underbody that moved easily for its bulk in calm water but suffered when wind and wave confronted its full bow. Judging by the distances Smith and crew made good with fair wind and tide, the barge performed well under certain points of sail, but it would not go to windward as well as modern craft, so the crew spent a good deal of time at the oars when conditions were less than ideal. Nonetheless, it proved seaworthy in carrying the crew through at least a couple of strong summer squalls but also was able to get into shallow places like Tangier Island (which Smith named Russell's Isles after Walter Russell, the expedition's first "doctor of physic") and sturdy enough to withstand bumping against rocks at the heads of navigation on the Susquehanna, James, and Rappahannock.

Indian craft on the Chesapeake were clumsier: large logs (preferably light and rot-resistant cypress and Atlantic white cedar) hollowed out by fire and scraping with shell tools, then shaped with squared-off, scowlike bows and sterns. The Indians learned through long experience to paddle and pole them well and to handle them in the Chesapeake's short, choppy seas. The only regional tribe with access to the breakthrough technology of frame-and-bark construction was the Massawomeck, whom Smith and crew encountered at the mouth of the Susquehanna during their second voyage up the bay in the summer of 1608.

The Indians knew their waters well, but the English were venturing into wild, unknown territory. They had no navigation charts, beyond rough sketches of maps that various natives had drawn in the earth with sticks for Smith. Smith's notebook held not only mapping

observations but also Indian words whose meanings Smith learned. He was a quick study and rapidly picked up the Alqonquian-based language of the Powhatan tribes. That facility became one of his most powerful tools.

One other point stands out in John Smith's explorations: the character of the men in the Virginia Colony. Despite the rigidly layered society of 17th-century England, they were a mixed lot, ranging from high-born gentlemen to common craftsmen and soldiers of fortune like Smith. They also ranged from industrious to slothful, heroic to selfish. On his various explorations and trading missions, Smith chose his crew not by lineage but by competence and willingness to work. He was a thoroughly democratic leader who saw that the colony could survive only by the exercise of those characteristics. Little did he know that this political philosophy would echo around the Chesapeake as representative democratic government developed over the succeeding four centuries.

Stores aboard the barge included barrels of water, bread, and dried meat, but there was never any promise of enough to last through the whole voyage. Thus the crew was absolutely dependent on living off

WINDS AND WEATHER

Chesapeake Bay weather generally comes from the west. In spring and fall, mounds of cool, dense air (high-pressure systems) sweep in from that direction, setting off rain. Sometimes, though, a low-pressure system that forms in the southwestern United States rides across Texas. Its counterclockwise rotation sweeps moisture from the Gulf of Mexico up into the southeastern states. That low may move through the Carolinas to drop substantial moisture on Virginia and Maryland before moving off the coast. Either way, southerly breezes give way to strong northwest winds rotating clockwise around the succeeding high-pressure system. During these two seasons of changing weather, those winds can be strong and blow for several days.

Summer, by contrast, often brings a "Bermuda high," a large dome of high pressure in the Atlantic that blocks low-pressure systems from sliding into the Chesapeake. Sometimes strong weather systems break this block, but more often, the high brings relatively stable weather. Days can become stiflingly hot as the sun heats the land, but by afternoon that heated air begins to rise, bringing in a breeze from the south strong enough to cause whitecaps to develop.

More ominous, though, are afternoon thunderstorms like the ones that ambushed Captain Smith at Tangier and Bloodsworth Islands in June 1608. They occur when humid, sun-warmed air rises very fast, causing condensation of the moisture and powerful static electricity. These storms can produce dangerous wind, waves, and lightning for periods as short as half an hour, after which everything calms down again.

In winter, cold fronts drop down to the Chesapeake from Canada, bringing the densest air and lowest tides of the year. A strong front may bring a powerful, multiday northwest wind that literally "blows the water out of the Bay," especially if it coincides with a new or full moon.

A storm pounds the marshy shore south of Rock Hall, Maryland, near the Eastern Neck National Wildlife Refuge.
DETAIL: *Sea vessel of Smith's time, taken from a contemporary account.*

the land and water. When in the company of friendly natives, they ate and drank well, but at other times they went thirsty and hungry, frequently while being shot at by Indian archers bent on killing them. Keeping up their energy for rowing was a constant challenge. Besides hostile humans, there were other forces threatening them, including bad weather and New World diseases.

To complete such explorations, John Smith had to be a strong and shrewd leader, exercising superb small-boat seamanship while exhorting his men to extraordinary effort and inspiring their loyalty. He succeeded partly because he was willing to work as hard and bear at least as much discomfort, thirst, and hunger as they and partly by his skill at dealing with the natives. He did not necessarily wish the latter ill, but he was bound and determined to carry out the orders of his employer, the Virginia Company, and he would not allow them to deter him. It is interesting to compare him with other explorers who left more complete records. A good one is Captain Meriwether Lewis, a Virginian who came along two centuries later to explore the Missouri and Columbia Rivers in the employ of President (and Virginian) Thomas Jefferson, putting to final rest the question of a Northwest Passage that Smith had sought in 1607-09. Though different in many respects, the men had similar leadership qualities and military skills, and they had to confront similar challenges.

In Smith's time, the Chesapeake's deeply forested watershed, opposite, acted as a "great green filter" for rain water, cleansing it and releasing it slowly to creeks, rivers, and the bay. Today, a number of restoration programs focus on restoring that watershed to its original state.

EXPLORATION TODAY

*F*or today's explorers, the Chesapeake is different, and so are we. Smith's "faire Bay" has attracted us humans like a huge, powerful magnet. Since 1607, the watershed's population has swelled by an astounding 16,000 percent, to 16 million, and it is now increasing by 100,000 per year, the same number as the total population in John Smith's time. Today, virtually all of the virgin timber in the watershed, the bay's "great green filter" of 1607, has been cut, though reforestation and land conservation have increased forest cover steadily since the low point in the mid-19th century. More problematic, though, is that nearly 15 percent of the watershed's 64,000 square miles has been covered by impervious surfaces—asphalt, concrete, and rooftops. The steady diet of nitrogen and phosphorus to which the bay ecosystem had adjusted has now swollen by an average of 600 percent, a supersized diet equivalent to taking an adult human from 3,000 calories per day to 18,000. Sources include wastewater, agricultural runoff, stormwater from urban and suburban areas, and emissions from vehicle exhaust and power plants.

That diet has fed explosive blooms of algae, which grow and cloud the waters, reducing light that the vital underwater grasses need to thrive and reproduce. The algae cells die fast and sink to the bottom, where massive populations of bacteria decay them, in the process driving down dissolved oxygen to levels that can be lethal to fish, crabs, oysters, and other bottom dwellers. Meanwhile, sediment runoff from cleared land has clogged river channels, smothered benthic (bottom) communities, and further clouded the waters. Heavy harvests of fish, shellfish, and water-fowl have dropped these animals' numbers to perhaps 10 percent of what they once were. In the words of Pogo, the comic strip possum of the 1950s and '60s, "We have met the enemy, and he is us." Clearly we are the most invasive species in this ecosystem.

How did we get from 1608 to today? The changes to the Chesa-peake ecosystem came slowly at first, mostly from the clearing of land for agriculture and timber harvest with iron implements and draft ani-mals, especially horses and oxen. Because tobacco depletes the soil quickly, raising it required lots of open land, with a significant percentage left fallow to recover in any given year. Harvesting of the Chesapeake's seafood increased with the use of iron tongs for gathering subsurface oysters and horses for pulling in haul seines. However, neither these efforts nor population growth was pervasive enough to unbalance the bay ecosystem.

Beginning around 1800, however, iron plows began biting deep into plantation soils, causing serious erosion. With steam power for sawmills, the clear-cutting of timber accelerated, causing more erosion. Formerly busy harbors on the rivers, such as Bladensburg on the Potomac's tributary Anacostia River, silted up and lost their shipping. As the industrial revolution took hold, first with water power and then with steam, population growth accelerated, as did the need for build-ing materials such as timber, sand, and gravel. Timber harvests also fueled home heating systems. Meanwhile, on the water, oyster dredges pulled by powerful sailboats mined oyster reefs down to depths of 50 feet, while haul seines grew to a mile or more in length, producing catches that were measured by bushels and boxes (100 pounds) rather than individual fish.

The first half of the 20th century brought widespread use of internal combustion engines and even more population growth.

Sewage, industrial wastewater, and stormwater joined more sediment
to pollute rivers with large urban centers, especially the Potomac
around the nation's capital, Washington, D.C. Catches of fish and oysters dropped, but not yet to catastrophic levels. By the end of World
War II, the population of the region had grown to eight million. With
postwar prosperity and increasing mobility courtesy of motor cars,
the population doubled to 16 million over the next 50 years, with
concomitant increases in pollution from a rapidly rising standard of
living. Harvest pressure on the bay's fish and shellfish—both commercial and recreational—grew with larger, faster boats with increasingly
sophisticated equipment, including fish-finding electronics. Stocks of
several species plummeted.

TIDES, CURRENTS, AND CHANNELS

 Compared with other Atlantic coast regions, diurnal (twice-a-day) tides in Chesapeake Bay are modest, varying from 1.5 feet on average around Baltimore to 4 feet up the Mattaponi River at Walkerton, Virginia. Spring tides on the new and full moons increase that value at Walkerton to nearly 5 feet.

Springtime snow melt or heavy rain from a tropical storm in central Pennsylvania can swell the Susquehanna and turn the upper bay into a raging torrent, as can the same conditions in the Shenandoah Valley into the Potomac. At those times, the river's flow can overpower the incoming tide, resulting in an ebb current lasting a day or more. Conversely, a strong coastal storm can push a storm surge of as much as eight feet up the bay and cause the high water to hang there for several days.

Similarly, strong northwest winds from powerful cold fronts can push water south, exposing channel banks three feet or more below a normal low tide. The shallow basin and large surface area of the Chesapeake render it especially susceptible to this wind effect.

In general, bay currents are strongest in narrow spots that force water to accelerate and weakest in broad sections. Typically, the current in those narrow spots also scours out deep grooves. In these locations and others like them, the momentum of a large volume of water can cause the current to keep moving even after the tide has reached its maximum or minimum height.

Most of the big rivers exhibit a series of sharp meanders in the middle of their tidal sections. In these turns, the water flows faster on the outside than on the inside. The outside currents (both flood and ebb) scour out the bank on that side, leaving deep water and firm land, while the slower ones on the inside allow sediments to settle, creating marshes and wooded swamps with shallow, muddy bottoms.

This view from the space shuttle Columbia *shows how the lower Chesapeake's tributaries weave their way through the surrounding lands. Today, they carry shipping and serve to delight a legion of recreational boaters.*
DETAIL: *A symbolic reference to strong winds, taken from Smith's 1612 map.*

Remarkably, however, there is much about the Chesapeake that is still "faire," and it is still the rich, dominant natural resource for the mid-Atlantic region in the country born of Smith's exploration and hard work. The past 25 years have seen a concerted effort to reverse the changes by many people who love the bay and want to see its health restored. In this work, we swim against the current of increasing population, but there are signs of progress to make us cautiously optimistic.

If these statements sound contradictory, so be it. The reality is that on any given day, you can find places around the Chesapeake that will make you smile for joy and others that will make you cry, often in proximity to each other. We hold fast to the wonderful even as we work to heal the damage.

There are still places along the Captain John Smith Water Trail that look roughly the way they did in 1607. This book will show you where to find and enjoy them. Even some of the most altered places, such as the Patapsco River at Baltimore Harbor, the Potomac at Washington, D.C., and the Elizabeth River between Norfolk and Portsmouth, show signs of Smith's bay, if you learn where to look.

The vessels at our disposal for exploring the John Smith trail are far more comfortable than the captain's *Discovery Barge*. The variety of water on the trail makes parts of it suitable for kayaks, canoes, good rowing boats, cruising sailboats, outboard skiffs, runabouts, and cruising powerboats, including trawlers. In addition to compasses and modern navigational charts (direct descendants of Smith's 1612 map), we have marine electronics that were unimaginable to Smith. Even kayaks now carry waterproof GPS plotters, handheld VHF radios, and cell phones. Food and water are readily available and easy to pack aboard. We still face weather issues like cold fronts and thunder squalls, but weather forecasts and other modern tools have taught us much about how to deal with the challenges the Chesapeake presents to us.

As a Virginia native and longtime field educator for the Chesapeake Bay Foundation, I have had the privilege of exploring most of these waters in a broad range of boats. As we near the 400th anniversary of Smith's voyages of exploration, there is much still here to delight and fascinate us, teach us how much the Chesapeake ecosystem wants to live and thrive, and inspire us to join the effort to restore it, for ourselves and for the generations of explorers that will follow us. Come join with us as we follow in Captain John Smith's wake.

As the sun rises in the east, watermen from Tangier Island, Virginia, pull up the trap end of a pound net. This hundred-yard-long net system is a direct descendant of the weirs that the Indians taught the English settlers to fish with four centuries ago. Tangier men have fished with them since they settled the island from Cornwall, England, in the mid-17th century.

Chapter Two

The second of June, 1608, Smith left the fort to perform his discovery…in an open barge near three tons burthen, leaving the Phoenix at Cape Henry, they crossed the bay to the eastern shore and fell with the isles called Smith's Isles after our captain's name.

— CAPTAIN JOHN SMITH,
General History, Book 3, Chapter 5

Tidal freshwater marshes like this one on Virginia's Chickahominy River near Jamestown served as "breadbaskets" for the bay's Indians, and their cypress trees furnished lumber for dugout canoes.

PRECEDING PAGES: *Three gulls soar over the broad mouth of the Chesapeake Bay near Cape Henry, Virginia. It was on a morning like this in April 1607 that the Jamestown colonists made their first landing on the beach nearby and named it for a son of their king.*

Storms, Marshes, and Indians

Although the Virginia Company of London had directed the Jamestown colonists to explore the Chesapeake, to determine the strength and trading potential of the Native Americans and especially to find the fabled Northwest Passage to the Orient, the colonists' primary objective during the first year was simply survival. The settlement was beset by disease, ineffective leadership, bickering, and unwillingness to adapt to the nature of the Jamestown environment.

During the summer of 1607, the expedition's leader, Captain Newport, had gone to England with two ships, leaving Captain Smith in charge of Indian negotiations. Smith had established a pattern of fair but firm dealing with the Indians in the Chesapeake area. The area was controlled by Powhatan, the paramount chief of more than 30 tribes. Though there was some infighting between tribes, Powhatan was widely respected and feared among the 20,000 Indians that the tribes comprised.

In December 1607, Captain Smith took the *Discovery Barge* to explore the nearby Chickahominy River. Powhatan's warriors captured him well upriver and marched him as a captive around the headwaters of the Chickahominy, Pamunkey, and Mattaponi Rivers, up to the village of Toppohannock on the Rappahannock, and back to Powhatan's capital, Werowocomoco, on the Pamunkey (today's York River). There, according to Smith's 1624 *General History,* Powhatan sentenced him to death by beating after he refused to acknowledge the chief as ruler of the colonists. At this point, Powhatan's favorite daughter, 10-year-old Pocahontas, threw herself on Smith and begged her father to spare his life. Moved by his daughter's display, Powhatan made Smith a *werowance,* a king or chief (and therefore, in his mind, an ally and subject).

In January 1608, Powhatan released him to return to Jamestown, where he worked through the spring helping to build and fortify the

colony and to find food for its inhabitants. He also made one trip back to Werowocomoco to introduce Captain Newport, who had returned with a new group of colonists to augment the originals, to Powhatan and to trade for corn.

In late May, Captain Smith picked a crew of 14 to accompany him on an expedition up the Chesapeake in the *Discovery Barge.* They included Walter Russell, the "doctor of physic," six gentlemen, and seven soldiers, including a "fisher," a fishmonger (who was presumed to know which fish were good to eat), a blacksmith, and a tailor (whose sewing skills would soon play an important role in the mission). One of the soldiers was the able and loyal Anas Todkill, who also wrote much of the log for the two voyages that Smith and the barge would undertake that summer.

SETTING SAIL

On June 2, 1608, the ship *Phoenix,* which had brought the new colonists, departed Jamestown with the *Discovery Barge* in tow. For the sailing vessels of this era, the twists and bends of the lower James River presented significant challenges in the forms of changing winds and powerful currents that could be friend or foe. The trip downriver to Hampton Roads and the mouth of the Chesapeake took all day. Even if the ship, barge, and crew had left Jamestown early in the day with a fair, ebbing tide, the current would have turned on them as they neared Hampton Roads. Moreover, a wind from the north would have helped them in the lower river but opposed them as they made their way out of Hampton Roads into the main body of the Chesapeake. A southerly wind would have produced the opposite effect. "Clear sailing" for a full day was a rare occurrence for 17th-century vessels in this estuary.

The James is a powerful river, carrying the third heaviest flow of fresh water in the bay system (after the Susquehanna and the Potomac). It rises out in southwestern Virginia, on the edge of the Allegheny Plateau, and flows several hundred miles east, reaching its falls and sea level at present-day Richmond, which grew up as the port at the head of navigation. The upper tidal section flows through meandering channels past the mouths of the river's two major tributaries, the Appomattox and the Chickahominy.

Jamestown itself lies on the outside of a meander, where the river is deep close to the bank—hence the choice of location for a

In this detail from Captain John Smith's map of 1612, opposite, the paramount chief Powhatan sits on an elevated bench in his longhouse at Werowocomoco, on the Pamunkee (today's York) River. Surrounding him are his werowances (chiefs) and his wives. Smith describes this scene when he was first brought before Powhatan as a prisoner in January 1608.

settlement. The next one downstream includes a marsh on the south side that would soon be named Hog Island as later colonists allowed their animals to live and forage there. Today, the marsh is a wildlife management area operated by the Virginia Department of Game and Inland Fisheries as a waterfowl refuge.

In 1608, the James's wooded watershed and extensive wetlands filtered runoff, so its waters were much clearer than they have been for the past two centuries. During that time, deep plowing for agriculture and urban/suburban development have clouded the river with sediment, especially the red clay soils from the Piedmont region above the falls.

Below Hog Island, at Burwell's Bay, the river's increasing salinity begins to produce shoals that in Smith's time were giant oyster reefs, breaking the surface and creating hazards to navigation. They extended all the way down into Hampton Roads, between modern-day Hampton/Newport News

Across the Chesapeake Bay's mouth from Cape Henry is Cape Charles, the southern tip of the Eastern Shore. The Jamestown colonists named it after King James's other son. Today it is part of the Eastern Shore National Wildlife Refuge.

to the north and Norfolk/Portsmouth to the south. In Smith's time, they served as major food sources for both natives in the village of Kecoughtan and colonists living at Point Comfort.

Eddies in this part of the river naturally cause the larvae produced by spawning oysters to stay in the area, making it arguably the best producing area for seed (young) oysters on the entire East Coast for the late 19th and 20th centuries. The reefs gave rise during that era to the watermen's communities of Menchville, to the north on Deep Creek (now part of the city of Newport News) and Rescue to the south, just inside the mouth of the lovely, marshy Pagan River, which leads up to the charming, restored town of Smithfield. The towns remain, as do a few of the watermen, but overharvesting, pollution, and disease have decimated the reefs. Smithfield today is a destination for yachtsmen, while Menchville becomes suburban and Rescue hangs on by its teeth.

Beaches at the mouth of the Chesapeake receive all sorts of gifts from the waves that break on them. Well-polished oyster shells showing many colors, like these, are common, but the moon snail at the lower left has washed in from deeper water.

At nightfall on that late spring day 400 years ago, the *Discovery Barge*'s crew boarded her at the mouth of the Chesapeake. The *Phoenix* cast off the towline and stood out into the Atlantic to return to England. At this point, scholars believe, Smith headed north overnight for what is now Cape Charles and landed at dawn on the low, marshy beach, now part of the Fisherman's Island National Wildlife Refuge, the northern terminus of the Chesapeake Bay Bridge-Tunnel.

Captain and crew made their way three miles to the northeast and explored a low barrier island that Smith named for himself. Today Smith Island, not to be confused with Maryland's Smith Island upbay, is part of the Nature Conservancy's Virginia Coast Reserve. Though Smith's journals say little about "Smith's Isles," a look at his map reveals clear particulars here but none farther north. This is another case, as Smith scholar Edward Wright Haile says, of "putting his details in the map instead of the book." In fact, the signatories to the account in Smith's *General History* are Dr. Walter Russell, Anas Todkill, and Thomas Momford, one of the gentlemen.

Returning into the Chesapeake, the explorers encountered "two grim and stout savages upon Cape Charles, with long poles like javelins headed with bone." After demanding "what we were and what we would," they became friendly and directed the explorers to Accomack (actually near the site of today's town of Cape Charles, not Accomack), to their *werowance.* The chief treated them kindly

SPRING

 The key to understanding spring on the Chesapeake Bay and its rivers is understanding the role of water's high specific heat. Physicists use this term to describe how much heat a material must absorb for its temperature to rise by one degree Celsius.

The term sounds arcane, but what it tells us is that water must absorb a lot of heat from the springtime sun before it warms up. Many cold-blooded Chesapeake creatures such as rockfish and blue crabs winter in deep water in the bay's main stem and lower tidal rivers, because the temperature there remains stable through the winter. In spring, though, those large volumes of water change temperature slowly, warming from the surface down. Fish such as spot, croakers, and summer flounder that have wintered in the Atlantic on the continental shelf (another area of stable water temperature) begin slowly to move toward the bay's mouth. Crabs also emerge from the mud bottoms where they have buried for the winter and begin foraging around.

Meanwhile, shallow coves and creeks warm quickly on sunny days, especially if they have southern exposure and dark, muddy bottoms. They cool down just as quickly at night, however. The first of the fish to start moving in the spring in these areas are the locals including yellow and white perch and several species of minnows, plus transients such as herring, shad, and rockfish that are swimming upstream to spawn.

As spring progresses, all of this activity will swell to a peak in May and early June, as the springtime spawners head back out to the Atlantic and the summer fish take up residence to feed in Chesapeake waters through the summer. Remember how water's specific heat "works" and you'll be able to follow this rich parade through the season.

A tidal marsh on the Nanticoke shows trees just beginning to "green up," including four red maples growing as wetlands plants. The aquatic plants in the foreground are just-emerged yellow pond lilies, and the dark green plants behind them are sweetflag. DETAIL: *Flora of the New World, drawn by a contemporary of Smith's.*

and spoke the Powhatan language, of which Smith had improved his knowledge during his captivity the previous winter. He described the bay shore to the north, leading Smith and his men to explore the inlets and creeks of what is now Virginia's bayside Eastern Shore, which the chroniclers described as "good for barks [barges] but not for ships." Meanwhile, Smith took enough notes to depict them with remarkable accuracy.

Today, the inlets and creeks look much the same. The Coriolis forces generated by Earth's rotation cause the clear, cold seawater entering the bay from the Atlantic to hug this shoreline, so water quality is generally good, and fish and shellfish still abound here. The southern portion of this shoreline includes beaches and, in a few places, surprising sandy bluffs, but to the north, from the mouth of Nandua Creek onward, the bay shore is increasingly marshy, dominated by saltmarsh cordgrass at the water's edge and salt meadows on the higher marsh. At least a dozen tidal creeks enter the bay directly. Smith would have explored the nooks and crannies of these creeks in search of blue crabs, speckled trout, and views of water birds such as ospreys and great blue herons. Today, local watermen, anglers, and paddlers do the same.

UP THE POCOMOKE

*S*eeing islands several miles offshore of the mainland (probably today's Watts and Tangier), Smith directed the barge's helmsman to steer for them, but one of the Chesapeake's legendary summer squalls ambushed them and they returned to sheltered waters on the mainland, probably in the vicinity of today's Chesconessex Creek. Short of drinking water, they followed "the next eastern channel" into the Pocomoke River, which was known then as the Wighcocomoco (Wicomico), a name that appears in at least five Chesapeake waterways, including two a few miles to the north. The natives at first threatened but then became friendly.

Despite the Indians' help, the explorers spent two days searching to find only three kegs of muddy water and then a "pond" of fresh water as warm as a bath, possibly well up in the Pocomoke's cypress swamps. That bathwater would be no surprise for anyone today who prowls this area in summer, even up that beautiful, tree-lined river. The water is clear but stained by tannins from the decaying bark and needles of the river's bald cypress trees.

Sanderlings are among the dozen or so shorebird species that live and feed along the sandy shores of Tangier Sound. They may look tiny and comical foraging between waves, but for their size, they are tough and powerful.

OPPOSITE PAGE:

These dunes at Cape Henry show the effects of wind on sand, as well as the beach-stabilizing capacity of American beach grass. Dunes like these serve as powerful shock absorbers for the energy thrown ashore by wind and waves, but the Indians of the Chesapeake region had little use for them as food sources.

Smith's map indicates that he went up the "Wighcocomoco" as far as modern-day Pocomoke City, where he placed one of his brass crosses to claim the land for the English crown. Above, the river runs through a corridor of bald cypress rimmed by lily pads. One large tributary, cypress-lined Nassawango Creek, enters the Pocomoke on the west side between Pocomoke City and Snow Hill. Much of its shoreline has been preserved by the Maryland Chapter of the Nature Conservancy. Both towns were important regional ports from the 18th century until World War II, especially for schooners and work-boats carrying cypress lumber to Baltimore and Norfolk. It took marvelous skill for a schooner captain to bring his 60- to 100-foot unpowered vessel up to Snow Hill to load lumber and then pilot it back down.

LIMBO

After descending the Pocomoke, Smith and his crew probably made their way across Pocomoke Sound and through shallow Cedar Straits to Tangier Sound. Today, you'll see a Virginia-Maryland state line marker in those straits, with Maryland's Cedar Island Wildlife Management Area to the north and the Chesapeake Bay Foundation's Great Fox Island education center to the south in Virginia. Storms gnaw relentlessly at all of these islands, so the outlines today differ from what Smith and his crew saw.

The accuracy of Smith's map indicates that as they headed up Tangier Sound, the barge and crew followed the mainland, mapping the Big Annemessex River, Deal Island, Monie Bay, and the Wicomico River. Late in the afternoon of June 6, they encountered an even worse squall, which blew out their foresail, dismasted the barge, and nearly sank the boat. They bailed with their hats and managed to find their way to today's Bloodsworth Island, where the storm pinned them down for two days, with very little cover except a few ridges of loblolly pine surrounded by salt marsh. (Smith's map shows a large island that may have been a combination of today's rapidly eroding South Marsh and Bloodsworth. This part of the Eastern Shore is actually subsiding, or sinking, even as sea level rises, so the island topography has changed considerably since 1608.)

The weather was bad enough that they named the place Limbo, after the supposed holding place for people destined for hell. John Powell, the tailor, now became the hero, repairing the sail with his mates' shirts. Somehow, the crew either salvaged their old mast or found a tree to shape a new one.

Today we might wonder what they ate and how they coped with the myriad biting insects, especially mosquitoes, greenheads, no-see-ums, mayflies, and sheep flies, that frequent Bloodsworth and other islands in the vicinity. The chroniclers make no mention of insects, nor do they describe Bloodsworth's marsh guts, creeks, shorelines, and rich eelgrass beds that provide habitat for shoals of blue crabs, rockfish, speckled trout, Atlantic croakers, Norfolk spot, flounder, oysters, and other bay delicacies that Richard Keale (the fishmonger) and Jonas Profit (the fisher) might have procured for them.

Tangier is the only inhabited offshore complex of islands in Virginia's portion of the Chesapeake. Just to the north in Maryland lies the aforementioned Smith Island (also a complex of low, marshy islands and whose name bears no connection to the captain), which claims the same distinction for that state. The truth is that while both Tangier and Smith have growing tourist trades, their economies still depend primarily on the bay's resources, which are shrinking. Crabs continue as the mainstay fishery, but their population has teetered on the edge of serious problems for at least a decade, while the decline of oysters in the 1990s dealt a crippling blow to watermen and their families who depended on them for winter income.

Visitors to these islands, though, are still able to fish both shallow and deep water and to watch the birds, especially shorebirds, pelicans, and herons (up to eight species) in spring and summer, augmented by waterfowl in the fall. Tangier Sound remains one of the most fascinating sections of the Chesapeake. It is no accident that the Chesapeake Bay Foundation operates four residential education centers here, on Port Isobel Island next to Tangier, on Great Fox Island, in the village of Tylerton on Smith Island, and at Bishops Head on Hooper Strait, opposite Bloodsworth Island. The natural settings of these centers provide powerful hands-on bay experience to thousands of students, teachers, and other adults each year.

The Nanticoke

*W*ith the Barge repaired and the weather more favorable, the crew headed back east toward the Eastern Shore mainland and "fell with a pretty, convenient river . . . called the Cuskarawaok" (today the Nanticoke). The mouth of the river is broad, and as did the *Phoenix* in the lower James, the *Discovery Barge* and her crew had to

PAGES 60-61:
At sunrise, great blue herons perch in their rookery on Tangier Sound's Bloodsworth Island. Captain Smith and his crew named this island Limbo because of the unpleasant days they spent there after a nasty thunder squall, while the crew's tailor, John Powell, repaired the Discovery Barge's *sails with parts of their (and presumably his) shirts. The herons find the island much more hospitable than did the English.*

Springtime red maple shoots and swamp azaleas, opposite, sprout from soil collected in a crevice at the base of a cypress tree on the Pocomoke River.

pick their way through large oyster reefs in the vicinity of today's Roaring Point.

The local natives proved less hospitable than the Accomacks, running along the east bank and howling, despite the crew's gestures of friendship. "They were not sparing of their arrows nor the greatest passion they could express of their anger." Smith wisely kept the barge to the center of the river, out of bow shot from either side, for the night.

In the morning, some Indians came to the beach with baskets and began to dance, inviting the English to join them. Sensing treachery, Smith ordered a volley of shot that dispersed them into a nearby marsh, where warriors were hiding in ambush. Late in the day, the crew approached the shore, firing more shots into the marsh. They found baskets and blood but no people.

Seeing smoke across the river, on the broad marsh that is today's Elliott's Island Wildlife Management Area, the crew rowed there and found fires burning beside several small houses but, again, no people. This would have been Nause, the village (or fishing/hunting camp) nearest the river's mouth. They left some of their trading goods—"copper, beads, bells, and looking glasses"—and made their way out of the river into Fishing Bay. At dusk, they returned to the middle of the river for the night.

The next morning, four Indians who had been fishing in the sound came by, not knowing what had happened the day before. The barge crew "used [them] with such courtesy" that they bade the English stay. They went away and quickly returned with "some twenty more" and then "two or three thousand men, women, and children [more likely several hundred]…clust'ring about us, everyone presenting us with something which a little bead would so well requite that we became such friends they would contend who should fetch us water, stay with us for hostage, conduct our men any whither, and give us the best content."

Anas Todkill and other chroniclers considered these natives "the best merchants of all other savages." Living in a narrow part of the Eastern Shore gave them easy access to the Atlantic, where they collected small sea shells much in demand as trade goods with other Indians from the north. The result was that the Nanticoke had the finest furs that Smith and the crew saw in their travels, not from the local marshes and woods but from colder north climates.

There is a mystery here. Smith's map records details of the Nanticoke's meanders that remain accurate today, but the chronicles make no mention of where and how the captain and crew traveled the river with

OPPOSITE PAGE:
A swallowtail butterfly sips nectar from a blossom. Flowers in the Chesapeake's marshes attract a dozen species of butterfly. They are particularly fond of swamp milkweed.

A praying mantis, below, eyes its prey. These powerful predators undoubtedly helped to quell insect pests in Indian vegetable gardens along the Chesapeake's rivers.

HERONS AND OSPREYS

 Two of the Chesapeake's best loved birds get very busy in the spring. Great blue herons, which have been picking out a solitary and meager living of killifish ("bull minnows") on south-facing mud banks up and down the Chesapeake system all winter, head for isolated but wooded islands and creeks to nest in raucous rookeries that range from a dozen to several hundred mated pairs. Meanwhile, hundreds of ospreys return from their "other summer" in Central and South America to nest with their mates on navigation markers, duck blinds, dead trees, and other elevated structures—both natural and man-made—up and down the bay and its rivers.

These two species of skillful fishermen ply their trades in different ways, to which each is beautifully adapted. The long-legged heron stalks the softest marsh mud on three-toed, eight-inch-long wading shoes. When it spots a fish, it freezes with its long neck coiled like a snake's body, peering intently at its quarry with sharp eyes. It strikes, spearing the fish with its long, lance-like bill, then flips it into the air and swallows it.

By contrast, the even sharper-eyed osprey strikes from the air, hovering to mark its prey, then folding its wings in a power dive while remaining tightly focused on the fish. It hits the water with a loud splash, locks its sharp talons into the fish's shoulder muscles, and works its prize aloft with its powerful, V-shaped wings. Twenty feet over the water, it pauses in flight to shake itself as a dog does after swimming, then flies away to eat its catch or deliver it to the family.

Between nest repair, egg laying, incubation of eggs, and feeding young, both great blue herons and ospreys will be active and visible around their nests and in their feeding areas throughout the spring and summer. They offer must-watch shows for bay explorers.

In late spring, an osprey stands guard over its two hatchlings in a nest built on an abandoned wire-mesh crab pot on a Tangier Sound marsh. Within two months, these young birds will grow to the size of their parents, learn to fly, and begin to fish.
DETAIL: *A bird in flight, from a 16th-century engraving.*

A *bullfrog emerges from a carpet of duckweed in a marsh pool along the upper Nanticoke. These large amphibians thrive in the freshwater sections of many Chesapeake rivers.*

OPPOSITE PAGE:

A *painted turtle surveys the scene from a favorite waterside log. This is the most brightly colored among the Chesapeake's two dozen terrestrial, aquatic, and marine species of turtle.*

their hosts. After much debate, archaeologists, historians, and land-use planners, equipped with modern Geographic Information Systems, now agree that they went up the main stem of the river to the mouth of Broad Creek, which lies a couple of miles over the present-day state line in Delaware, and placed a brass cross there. They may also have traveled into the Nanticoke's large northwest tributary, Marshyhope Creek. There were settlements all along both waterways, especially in the area between modern-day Vienna, Chicone Creek, and the mouth of the Marshyhope, which some scholars believe was the site of the chief's village, Kuskarawaok, as shown on Smith's map.

There is a good chance that the river people invited Smith and his men to ride in their canoes, which were faster than the *Discovery Barge,* to explore their home territory. Because the English were in the river only a couple of days, they must have covered a lot of territory in a hurry if the map truly represents first-hand exploration. More likely, it shows a combination of water time and information gained from the natives.

By Indian protocol, the time would also have included at least one feast with a chief. The area in question is far enough upriver that the marshes in the vicinity all grow low-salinity plants such as wild rice, arrow arum, and arrowhead, which fed the Native Americans in the fall and winter, as well as attracting thousands of migratory water-fowl. At this earlier season, meals would have consisted of game, such as deer and wild turkey.

Both the Nanticoke and the Marshyhope remain remarkably wild and beautiful today, with wooded shorelines and swamps, marshes full of birds, and small creeks begging for exploration. It is not difficult to understand why Harriet Tubman found these swamps and marshes useful for her trips along the 19th century's Underground Railroad. Since then, much of the land has been managed for commercial timber, and some is now preserved. The small Maryland river towns of Vienna and Sharptown were shipping and shipbuilding centers during the 18th and 19th centuries, as was tiny Bethel, Delaware, five miles up Broad Creek. Since freight and passengers forsook the river for the highways, they have languished, though Vienna and Bethel are working to reinvent themselves as towns with a strong sense of community and history.

Farther upstream on the main river, a sand and gravel pit, a fuel oil terminal, and DuPont's first nylon plant at Seaford, Delaware, keep that small city tied to the river, with a remnant of water transportation in the form of tugs pushing barges. Meanwhile, the Marshyhope also

remains little changed, though Federalsburg survives as the town at the head of navigation.

The Nanticoke drains cypress and bottomland hardwood swamps in large portions of Sussex County, Delaware, and Dorchester, Wicomico, and Caroline Counties in Maryland, making it another powerful Chesapeake river. Below Vienna, the outsides of the curves show 50 feet of water, and there is more than 40 feet at Red Bank, the first hard turn on the north bank of the Marshyhope going upstream. The tides actually have higher vertical fluctuations, and the currents run stronger up the Chesapeake's tidal rivers—including this one—than down at the mouths. As on the James, town sites like Vienna's are invariably located on the outside of river bends.

In the spring, a boat with a depth sounder will "see" thousands of fish moving upriver to spawn: rockfish (striped bass), white perch,

American shad, hickory shad, alewife herring, blueback herring, yellow perch, and even Atlantic sturgeon. Smith would have known all of these. At one time, watermen harvested large catches from the Nanticoke, but today only a couple of families fish the river commercially. Recreational anglers, however, find a mix of rock, perch, large mouth bass, and channel catfish from Vienna up, with more rock, spot, croakers, and gray trout in the lower reaches. Other fishers along the river include ospreys in season (March through August), and bald eagles and river otters year round.

Beautiful as it is, though, the Nanticoke unfortunately today suffers a heavy human footprint. Suburbia is spreading out rapidly from the commercial center of Salisbury, Maryland. Much of the non-swamp or timber land is cultivated for grain or given over to chicken houses that raise millions of broilers each year. Sewage, suburban stormwater, and farm runoff fill the river with sediment and nitrogen/phosphorus pollution that fuels explosive algae blooms. Much is being done to improve sewage treatment and help farmers reduce the river's burden of nitrogen and phosphorus, but the lower part of the Nanticoke still tends to run thick and brown today, not clear as in Smith's time.

North to the Patapsco

*D*espite the trading abilities of the Nanticoke people, Smith saw little potential for profit to the Virginia Company there. He did, however, listen as they "much extolled a great nation called Massawomekes" who lived far to the north but traded high-quality furs with them. Here was a clue to what Smith was looking for: furs and that fabled Northwest Passage to the Orient. As soon as he could politely do so, he bade the Nanticokes farewell, gathered his crew, and headed the Discovery Barge downriver to search for the Massawomekes.

They passed out of the broad river mouth, by Fishing Bay and through Limbo (Hooper) Strait, past Bishops Head, where the CBF's Karen Noonan Center for Environmental Education stands today. Beyond the strait, they sailed by the Honga River and Lower Hooper Island to the open Chesapeake. Smith's map shows these features, including a hint of the Transquaking River system at the head of Fishing Bay, and labels the tip of Lower Hoopers Island as Momford's Point (after Thomas Momford, who helped Russell and Todkill write the log).

A 17th-century French soldier in America, opposite, observed that Indian hunters skinned out large deer in one piece, so that they could wear the pelts, with the heads over their own and their eyes looking out. These disguises allowed them to stalk live deer very effectively, getting well within range for their powerful bows and arrows. In general, the Indians of the Chesapeake region were much more sophisticated than the English gave them credit for.

FOLLOWING PAGES: At dusk on a winter's day, a mist settles onto the Nanticoke near Riverton, Maryland. Except for the dock and a couple of houses, this section of the river looks much as it did in Smith's time.

Here they could just see the loom of the tall cliffs along the western shore above the mouth of the Patuxent, today known as Calvert and Scientist's Cliffs. They could probably also see the mouth of the Patuxent River, but with their minds set to the north, they ignored it for now. Sensing that the cliffs meant springs with good drinking water, wooded land with game, and the possibility of large rivers, they made straight for them and anchored under them for the night. They did indeed find the cliffs "well watered," as creeks running through deeply wooded ravines cut drains for rainwater every few miles. Accordingly, they filled their kegs, but they did not linger.

Over the next two days, the crew covered "30 leagues" (more like 100 miles), probably taking advantage of favorable wind and tide, since the barge made far better time under sail than oars. Focused on the western shore, they took little notice of the Choptank River, Eastern Bay, and the Chester River to the east. Perhaps Sharps, Poplar, and Kent Islands obstructed their views. On the map, Smith simply labels three amoeba-like blobs as Winston's Isles. Today, Sharps is gone completely, marked only by a tilting lighthouse, while Poplar, severely eroded, is being restored with dredge spoil from the approach channels to Baltimore Harbor. Kent Island endures, rapidly becoming a bustling Eastern Shore suburb of Annapolis.

Along the western shore, Smith mapped features such as Herring Bay and the South, Severn, and Magothy Rivers. He dismissed them as "many shallow creeks" but noted that while "very mountainous and barren," they held "valleys very fertile...much frequented by wolves, bears, deer, and other wild beasts." The log also notes that the crew were surprised to find no native people along this stretch. They would be stunned today by the settlement along these rivers in modern Calvert and Anne Arundel Counties, which bustle with more than half a million people as outer ring suburbs of Washington, D.C., and Baltimore. Even so, these rivers still have pockets of wildness, though a large fleet of recreational sail and power boats often obscures them.

Historians believe that Smith may have anchored the barge overnight in the Magothy, finding his way the next day into "the first inlet we found navigable for a ship [which] we called Bolus." This was today's Patapsco, which he explored as far upstream as Elkridge, leaving the barge at the falls to explore the interior and place a cross on a hill he marked on the map as "Blands C:". The Patapsco River serves as a starting point for the next chapter.

Scientist's Cliffs is part of a large formation of cliffs that reaches from just above the mouth of the Patuxent to Herring Bay, along Maryland's western shore. The ancestral Susquehanna carved them out during the last ice age, when sea level was more than 300 feet lower than it is today. The erosion exposed many marine fossils laid down some ten million years ago, during the Miocene epoch, when this area was covered by a shallow, warm sea.

Chapter Three

*R*egain therefore your old spirits, for return
I will not (if God please) till I have seen the
Massawomecks, found Patawomeck, or the head
of this water you conceit to be endless.

— CAPTAIN JOHN SMITH,
General History, Book 3, Chapter 5

Most people know Maryland's Patapsco River as an industrial waterway that leads to Baltimore Harbor. Parrs Spring, pictured here, is where the Patapsco begins its course to the Chesapeake Bay.

PRECEDING PAGES: *In the fall, trees along the Potomac near Great Falls provide a brilliant backdrop to the river's water and rocks. Smith and his crews saw scenes like this, mostly in other seasons, on the James, Rappahannock, Potomac, Patapsco, and Susquehanna Rivers.*

Searches for Gold

The "Bolus Flu:" was today's Patapsco River, which now is dominated by the city, port, and suburbs of Baltimore. The intervening 400 years have modified this area so much that it is difficult to conjure up what Smith and his men saw here. A look at the map reveals that he noted today's Rock and Curtis Creeks on the south side and Old Road Bay, Bear Creek, the Inner Harbor (also called the Northwest Branch), and Middle Branch to the north. On the main stem, Smith took the barge to the fall line, the site of the current town of Elkridge.

At this point, he and his crew tied off the barge, then climbed several miles up the steeply rising, deeply wooded land to the Blands C:, naming a nearby valley Downes Dale. During this exploration, the crew encountered no natives, so the river and tributaries on the map represent some combination of real explorations and surmises, especially in the headwaters. The presumption today is that the area was left alone by tribes to the south, as a buffer against the Susquehannock and Massawomeke. The crew's one tangible find was veins of red and white clay along the tidal shorelines at the high-water mark. This clay they suspected of being bole armoniac, which the English believed to have medicinal properties.

Today, more than a million people live in the watershed of the Patapsco. Jones Falls, the principal tributary of the Inner Harbor, rises as a trout stream north of the city in Baltimore County, but upon entering the city limits, it flows into a concrete-lined ditch that in turn gives way to a large concrete pipe that disciplines its course until it reaches the harbor. Meanwhile, that pipe gathers water from many city tributaries that we know as storm drains. Stormwater pollution is gradually taking over from industrial discharges as the primary source of pollution in the Patapsco, augmented by the flow from the region's

sewage treatment plants and spills of raw wastewater from cracks in the city's aging network of pipes, many of which date back to the early 20th century. Is Smith's Bolus Flue dead today? Not yet, but it has borne a heavy burden for three centuries. Here's a quick sketch of how the city and its surroundings evolved.

Smith was right about it being navigable for a ship. By the mid-17th century, the land was settled by English colonists to raise tobacco. As was true on most other large Chesapeake rivers, the head of navigation became a port. That would be Elkridge, and also true to form, the town grew up on the outside of a river bend, where the water was deepest. Today's Rolling Road marks the route by which farmers rolled hogsheads of tobacco to the docks with the aid of teams of oxen.

However, as on other upriver ports, tobacco farming fed the river a heavy diet of silt, which only grew greater with the introduction of deep plowing in the early 19th century and the growth of impervious surfaces (rooftops, roadways, and parking lots) in the 20th, accelerating the runoff of stormwater. Much of the upper Patapsco valley is now protected as a state park, but the damage to the lower channel restricts travel on it to canoes and kayaks.

Like Rolling Road, Reedbird Avenue on the south side of the river in today's unincorporated town of Brooklyn harks back to another era. Up until the late 19th century, the marshes on the Patapsco where Potee Street crosses it were filled with wild rice and other seed-producing marsh plants that attracted large fall migrations of reedbirds (bobolinks) and migratory waterfowl. Today, however, silt has smothered those marshes, and the rice has given way to the invasive *Phragmites* reed.

As Elkridge faded, the village of Baltimore on Jones Falls combined the stream's water power with its navigable channel. In the early 18th century, merchants began grinding local grain into flour and shipping it to Europe. Nearby deposits of high-grade sand and crude iron ore led to glass-blowing and smelting. Baltimore's access to the northern and western frontiers made it worthwhile for ships to sail up the bay, and the development of the Baltimore and Ohio Railroad in the 19th century made the city a central location for exporting both raw materials and manufactured goods, and for bringing in imports. Thus, it has flourished over the past three centuries, though today it and its port struggle to reinvent themselves as the city loses manufacturing jobs.

Anyone who explores the Patapsco today will at first be put off by the industrial-looking shoreline and the apparent lack of natural elements. But water quality has improved somewhat over the past 50 years, especially as the Clean Water Act of 1972 has eliminated the

OPPOSITE PAGE:
Reedgrass stands in frost on a wintry day near Cape Charles. The plant is native, but an invasive strain appeared around the Chesapeake in the last century, crowding out many native marsh plants on soils disturbed by human activity. The plant has some worth for stabilizing soil but, unfortunately, very little value for wildlife.

Red algae grow in the intertidal zone along a beach where wind and tidal currents have distributed black sand containing iron compounds. The Indian tribes around the Chesapeake learned how to use natural materials like these to decorate their faces, bodies, and clothes for a wide range of purposes.

most egregious point-source pollution from industrial and munic-
ipal wastewater. More recently, landmark legislation is accelerating
the upgrading of sewage treatment, and the city is replacing its
ancient pipes. Now there are pockets of natural shoreline, such as the
wetlands at Fort McHenry restored by volunteers and staff from the
National Aquarium in Baltimore, and the oyster reef at Fort Carroll,
just outside Key Bridge, which is being stocked by oysters grown by
students under the Chesapeake Bay Foundation's Oyster Corps program. Meanwhile, on any given day, other students learn from field
trips conducted aboard various indigenous workboats by CBF and the
Living Classrooms Foundation.

The Inner Harbor's working waterfront is quickly giving way to
restaurants and condominiums with marinas attached, giving the city a
booming business in recreational boating. From May through December,
several guides and a host of private anglers catch rockfish, white perch,
and other fish, while crabbers enthusiastically ply their trotlines.

Sadly, the Maryland Department of the Environment has had to
issue fish consumption advisories because of contamination by PCBs
and mercury. Thus, the Patapsco today is a mixture of both damage
and hope, as the river and its creatures stubbornly fight for their lives,
with some assistance from humans.

STIRRING WORDS

*F*or Smith and crew, the trip up the Bolus Flue was tiring. They had
to row most of the way in the June heat, they had been jammed together
in a small boat for two weeks, and the only food they had was bread
that had gone stale and was spoiled "by wet."

Now the crew began to beg Smith to return to Jamestown, in
spite of the fact that they had not achieved their objectives. Smith
responded eloquently:

> *You cannot say but I have shared with you in the worst,*
> *which is past. And for what is to come—of lodging, diet, or*
> *whatsoever—I am contented you allot the worst part to myself.*
>
> *As for your fears that I will lose myself in these unknown*
> *large waters, or be swallowed up in some stormy gust, abandon*
> *these childish fears, for worse that is passed is not likely [to] hap-*
> *pen, and there is as much danger to return as to proceed.*

*At Venice on the Bay, near
the mouth of the Patapsco
River, stones stabilize
the banks of a small creek,
opposite. Because the tidal
waters of the Chesapeake
system lie adjacent to the
unconsolidated clay, loam,
sand, and gravel soils
of the coastal plain, there
were no rocks here in John
Smith's time, but many
are brought to the bay and
its rivers today to stabilize
shorelines eroding because
of rising sea level.*

*FOLLOWING PAGES:
A whitetail doe and a
great blue heron share
a tidal fresh marsh on
the Patuxent River near
Upper Marlboro,
Maryland. Thanks to
state preservation efforts,
parts of the area look
much as they did when
Smith and crew visited
in the summer of 1608,
despite their proximity to
Washington, D.C.*

Regain therefore your old spirits, for return I will not (if God please) till I have seen the Massawomecks, found Pata-womeck, or the head of this water you conceit to be endless.

Two hen and three drake mallard ducks, opposite, stroll along a grassy Patapsco River shoreline opposite the former Bethlehem Steel plant at Sparrows Point. Though they look like wildlife, the mallards are descendants of pen-raised domestic birds and thus are common sights in suburban and even urban areas of the Chesapeake region.

The stirring speech revived the crew's spirits and strengthened their confidence in Smith as a leader, but then the wind and weather shut them in the Bolus Flue or the nearby Gunpowder, which added to their misery and caused several men to become "extreme sick." Finally, hearing their "pitiful complaints," Smith relented. When the wind lay down, the captain turned the *Discovery Barge* back down the bay. At this point, however, the captain and crew felt so refreshed that when they found the Potomac's broad mouth, they turned west and went up it.

Patawomeck, to which Smith had referred in his stirring speech, was a werowance town beside a large river on the northern fringe of Powhatan's confederacy, about which Smith had probably learned during his captivity the previous winter. Its outstanding attraction was *matchqueon*, a silvery substance that warriors mixed with grease to smear on their faces and bodies, "which makes them look like blackmoors dusted with silver." The Patawomeck people prized it highly. Suspecting that matchqueon might be silver and that the big river offered another opportunity to search for a Northwest Passage made Smith eager to investigate.

After making the difficult decision to turn back on the voyage up the Chesapeake, on June 16, "we fell with the River Patawomeck. Fear being gone and our men recovered, we were all content to take some pains to know the name of that seven mile broad river." Smith may have suspected what the river was from maps drawn by various natives, but remember that he made this seemingly paradoxical statement from hindsight 16 years later in the *General History.*

"For thirty miles' sail," he continued, "we could see no inhabitants." The lack of natives could easily have been due both to their desire to remain hidden and to the river's width. At the mouth of "a little bayed creek," they met two men who led them in. There they encountered an ambush, with "three or four thousand savages" (or "3 or 400" in Smith's earlier *Proceedings*).

Smith ordered a loud volley of shot that ricocheted off the water, causing a visual show of force and a booming echo from the surrounding woods. Terrified, the "ambuscados" threw down their bows and arrows and agreed to exchange hostages. Crewman James Watkins went with his captors "six miles up the woods to their king's habitation," Onawmanient (known today as Nomini). Smith notes, possibly in speculation, that "we were kindly used of those savages," whom Powhatan had commanded to attack them, "so directed by the discontents at James town." The wily Powhatan may have been delighted to follow this suggestion, since he had made Smith one of his werowances (and so his subject) upon the captain's release from captivity in January, and Smith had not asked the paramount chief's permission to go exploring through his territory.

From here, Smith's account requires some detective work. He speaks of "like encounters" in several places on the river but friendlier treatment in others. Until the section in the *General History* on the Rappahannock, Smith also neglects to describe the assistance of Mosco, "a lusty Salvage of Wighcocomoco," which was actually at the mouth of the Potomac (today's Little Wicomico River), in the area where Smith said they saw no natives at first. And he refers to an encounter at Cecawonee (Coan River), which is only about 15 miles above Wighcocomoco, and well below Onawmanient.

Thus we do not know where they encountered Mosco, but we know from the Rappahannock flashback that, unlike other natives,

SUMMER

 As the days lengthen and the sun's rays grow stronger, the warmth penetrates deeper into the waters of the Chesapeake and its tributaries. The small native fish such as white perch, the young of spring-spawning shad, herring, and rockfish, and overwintering young Atlantic croakers begin to move around. Blue crabs, mud crabs, and grass shrimp begin summer mating rituals.

The warming bay waters draw in fish that have wintered on the Atlantic's continental shelf, where the temperature has stayed warmer than the Chesapeake all winter and spring but will remain colder than the bay system will be all summer. (Remember the temperature "inertia" caused by water's high specific heat.)

The fish that enter the bay include some young-of-the-year spawned offshore in the fall, including Norfolk spot and menhaden. Mixing with young-of-the-river spawners, the overwinterers, and the crustaceans, they form a massive lower tier of the Chesapeake's food web, feeding rockfish, bluefish, flounder, Spanish mackerel, and larger members of the drum family that include red drum, gray trout (weakfish), speckled trout, and Atlantic croakers. Up the rivers, predator fish also include largemouth bass, chain pickerel, and white, channel, and blue catfish.

From the salt marshes of the lower Chesapeake to the wild rice marshes of the upper tidal rivers, plant growth accelerates to a peak in late August, producing lush vegetation in these rich communities that mark the transition from water to shore. In summer, they hum with life, especially including small fish seeking to evade larger ones. In fact, the plight of the fish grows even worse, thanks to daytime attacks from the air by ospreys, great blue herons, and gulls. At night, they must evade river otters. Summer is a busy time for all of the Chesapeake's creatures.

Marsh hibiscus flowers open to sunrise on a summer day along the upper tidal Potomac River. These crimson-centered blooms may be white or several shades of pink. They are prominent warm-weather symbols of the riches of Chesapeake river marshes.
DETAIL: *Trees from a 1590 book of engravings after John White.*

Mosco had a "blacke bush beard," which caused Smith and his crew to surmise that he was "some French mans son." He welcomed the similarly bearded English as brothers and assisted them in going upriver to Patawomeck, bringing them water and wood for fires, and cajoling his countrymen into towing the *Discovery Barge* "against wind and tide."

Under Mosco's direction, the route to Patawomeck may well have wandered to the north side of the river, since he would have known those people. Because they were not on Powhatan's tributaries, they might well have been friendly and willing to trade with the English. On his map, Smith notes a village at Nonanaukon (today's St. Clements Creek), the outline of what appears to be a combination

of St. Clements and St. Catherine's Islands with the small sound and White's Neck Creek behind. He also marked a King's House at Cecomocomoco (Wicomico River), a village at Potapaco on the Port Tobacco River, Nushemouck and Matquahquamend on either side of Nanjemoy Creek, and Nussantek opposite Patawomeck, which lay in the mouth of Potomac Creek, back in Powhatan territory. Smith implies that the Patawomeck people began by harassing him and then became friendly. He would have asked to see the matchqueon mine, but apparently the Patawomeck chief turned him down on this initial meeting.

This engraving, opposite, shows natives trading with colonists near a waterfront fur-drying encampment. Note the swap of an iron knife for furs in the foreground. Note also a sister of John Smith's Discovery Barge tethered to the stern of the ship at the center in the background.

Instead, Smith continued upriver, without Mosco. The Discovery Barge visited Pamacocack (both sides of the river), Cinquaoteck (today's Mattawoman Creek), Tauxanent (Occoquan River), Moyaones (Piscataway Creek), Namassingakent (Dogue Creek, home of the Toag people), Assaomeck (Hunting Creek), Natchotank (the mouth of the Anacostia River), and Namoraughquand (around the Rosslyn section of Arlington).

From there, Smith proceeded to the Potomac's fall line, "so high as we could with the boat," somewhere between today's Little Falls and Great Falls. There he and his crew encountered several canoes of natives "well loaden with the flesh of bears, deer, and other beasts, whereof we had part." It appears that the *Discovery Barge*'s crew not only ate well, thanks to these generous hunters, but also traded for furs.

Their main interest at the falls, however, was the rocks. "And divers places where the waters had fall'n from the high mountains they had left a tinctured, spangled scurf that made many bare places seem as gilded." Gold? Unfortunately not. "Digging the ground above the highest clifts of rocks [around Great Falls] we saw it was a clay sand so mingled with yellow spangles as if it had been half pin-dust [brass filings left from making pins]."

Smith turned back downriver instead, to ask the King of Patawomek again about the mine of matchqueon. This time, possibly having been persuaded by Mosco, the king offered guides and sent them to "a little river called Quiyough" (Aquia Creek), "up which we rowed so high as we could." There Smith left the barge, "six shot" (armed crewmen), and "divers salvages," and marched with the guides "seven or eight mile" to the mine, where they "digged a great hole with shells and hatchets." In a nearby "fair brook" they washed the ore and bagged it in the manner taught by their guides. "With so much as we could carry we returned to our boat, kindly requiting this kind king and all his kind people."

Later on, the matchqueon ore would prove to contain no silver, appearing instead to have been antimony, a metallic element. It is interesting, though, to speculate where the mine was. Aquia Creek straddles the fall line like most others that enter the Potomac River from the west, from Potomac Creek just below Aquia to Hunting Creek all the way up to Alexandria. Aquia's upper reaches flow down from elevations of at least several hundred feet above the Piedmont Plateau. It follows a meandering course to its head of navigation and soon forks above there.

Its northernmost branch, Beaverdam Run, is the longest, extending all the way to the point where today's Stafford, Prince William, and Fauquier Counties meet not far from the Blue Ridge Mountains. The elevation of Aquia's headwaters is about 350 feet above sea level. Though hardly a mountain, the land is high enough to give Captain John Smith and his guides some exercise on their way to the mine. These were tough people!

A THREATENED RIVER

Though the area's mineral riches were doubtful, the crew did find an abundance of wildlife. The woods and shoreline were teeming with bears, beavers, otters, minks, and wildcats. And there were so many fish, "lying so thick with their heads above the water," that the crew tried to catch them with frying pans. For some reason they had brought no nets, but they were tantalized by the nearness of the fish—of greater quantity and variety than the men had ever seen. "But they are not to be caught with frying pans!"

Alas, the fish are not nearly so abundant now. The Natchotank people at the mouth of the Anacostia River in Smith's time lived among some of the finest tidal fresh marshes in the entire Chesapeake, gathering not only wild rice and other food plants but also bountiful springtime runs of herring, shad, rockfish, and sturgeon. As English settlers moved in, they set their slaves to working the river for fish and waterfowl. The Port of Bladensburg, 12 miles up the river, prospered in shipping out tobacco. After the Civil War, the river became home for a tight-knit and skillful group of free African-American watermen.

Unfortunately, however, land clearing for tobacco culture in the Anacostia watershed led to destructive floods and heavy loads of sediment, which ruined the channel into Bladensburg. By the mid-19th century, it had lost its status as a major port. Meanwhile, engineers

In an upriver marsh, a spider spins its web from one grass stalk to another. In summer on the Chesapeake, spiders and dragonflies live well on insect diets. The spiders trap their prey at night in the webs they have spun, while the acrobatic dragonflies catch their prey in the air.

OPPOSITE PAGE:

In late summer, brown wild rice grains ripen on a tall green stalk in a tidal fresh marsh up one of the Chesapeake's rivers. Acres of wild rice grow in these marshes. It was a staple for the bay's Indians, as well as a valuable energy source for migratory waterfowl and other birds that stop to feed around the Chesapeake in the fall.

An Indian, opposite, preserves fish by smoking them. Their shape and underslung mouths indicate that they may be red drum, but native fishermen also smoked large quantities of American shad and herring when they ran up the bay's rivers in the spring of the year.

PAGES 96-97:
A great blue heron stretches its neck to spear a fish caught in an eddy below Great Falls on the Potomac. On their first voyage up the bay in the summer of 1608, Smith and his crew brought the Discovery Barge *all the way up to here, looking for gold and a Northwest Passage to the Orient.*

expanding the nation's capital after the war combined the city's sewer system with its stormwater pipes, causing raw sewage to overflow in heavy rainstorms right up till today. In the early 20th century, the U.S. Army Corps of Engineers decided to enclose the lower eight miles of the Anacostia's channel in concrete walls, then dredge the channel and use the spoil to fill in behind the walls. That was the end of the marshes, and the coup de grâce for the already declining spring runs of fish.

The explosive growth of the Washington metropolitan area over the 20th century created vast expanses of concrete and asphalt on both sides of the river, fouling the runoff of rainwater, while more and more people strained overloaded sewage treatment systems. In 1966, President Lyndon Johnson called the Potomac "a national disgrace." But the first Earth Day, in 1970, focused attention on it, and the Clean Water Act of 1972 began the slow process of restoring its health.

Gradually, the river began to turn around. By 1985, its underwater grasses began to come back. A world-class recreational fishery for largemouth bass developed around the grass beds, which also attracted migratory waterfowl. Bald eagles and ospreys returned to the river, as did rockfish, herring, and shad. Boaters began to ply the river again, sailing, paddling, cruising, fishing, and even windsurfing. Captain John Smith would find the changes to the shoreline unbelievable, but he would still recognize the rocky gorge between Little Falls and Great Falls, now protected by Virginia, Maryland, and the National Park Service.

Although the Potomac around Washington has again become a great natural resource for those who live there, it remains a threatened river, with millions of people living in its watershed. The massive Blue Plains sewage treatment plant, which serves the District of Columbia and parts of both Maryland and Virginia, has made great strides in cleaning up its discharges, but its outflow is so large that it constitutes a major bay tributary in its own right. Any failure in its treatment of several hundred million gallons of wastewater per day would be catastrophic for the river.

Meanwhile, heavy commuter traffic on area roadways and agricultural runoff from the river's busy watershed in Virginia, West Virginia, and Maryland adds to the pressure on it. The Anacostia remains the most badly damaged element in the Potomac system, but the District is beginning to think of it again as a resource, not something to hide and forget. It has been a great revelation to find that a major bay river like the Potomac can return from the dead, but the corollary lesson is that we can never take for granted the health of a river with several million people living around it.

As one travels farther from the Washington area, the lower Potomac looks more as it did when Smith explored it, though the mid-river counties like Stafford in Virginia and Charles in Maryland are dealing with heavy growth pressures themselves. Aquia Creek has three large marinas located near its mouth, houses all the way up to its head of tide, and large commuter subdivisions in its upper watershed around the matchqueon mine, but it also still holds some wide marshes. Nearby Potomac Creek contrasts waterfront houses with the still-wild Crow's Nest Peninsula, between its north shore and its tributary Accokeek Creek.

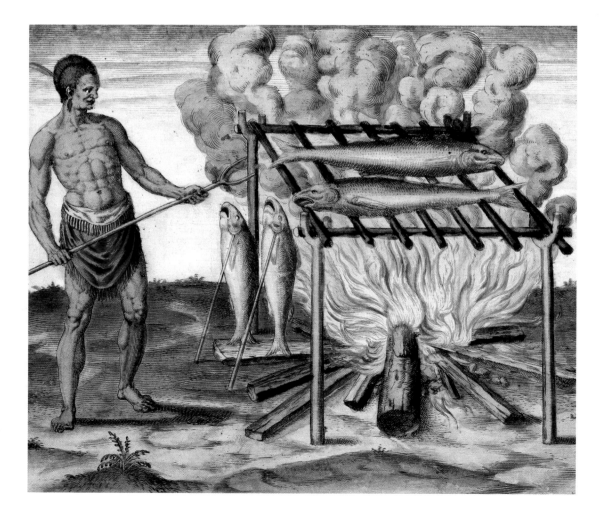

BLUE CRABS

Every rich ecosystem needs a full inventory of scavengers to take advantage of the biological debris that its food web leaves behind. The ultimate members of that team are bacteria, but an efficient, balanced system includes multiple tiers of scavengers that make the most of intermediate steps in the decay process.

The Chesapeake has plenty of scavengers, from large herring gulls through small mud crabs and seaworms to tiny, shrimplike amphipods. The best known and loved, however, is the blue crab. It's best not to ask what this tough, irascible critter eats, but it somehow manages to convert its diet of offal into succulent meat that is prized highly not only by humans but also by herons, speckled trout, raccoons, and a host of other aquatic animals.

Maryland has elevated blue crabs to the status of religious icons, and indeed they do grow well in that state's mid-salinity waters, but the truth is that the vast majority of them are born in Virginia. The reason is simple: The eggs require water of high salinity to hatch properly. Let the record show that crabs grow well in the mid-salinity portions of Virginia's rivers, too, but the bottom line is that this icon of the Chesapeake is a true bay creature that uses the whole estuary during its life cycle.

In fact, after the eggs hatch, they move toward light, bringing them up to the surface, where fresh water flowing out of the bay sweeps them out into the Atlantic. Then their attraction to light turns to repulsion, so they drop down into the deep, salty current that moves into and up the bay. They go through several larval metamorphoses in the underwater grass beds of the lower Chesapeake, make the critical transition to "first crab" stage there, and disperse throughout the main stem and the rivers, even up to the limit of tide.

A large jimmy (male) crab rests on the mud beside a stalk of saltmarsh cordgrass. Obvious in this photograph are the jimmy's large, powerful claws, the flat rear swimming legs, the complex mouth for eating a wide variety of food, and the crab's characteristic blue color.
DETAIL: *A Chesapeake crab, from a 16th-century engraving.*

Farther down, St. Marys County in Maryland and Westmoreland and Northumberland in Virginia largely retain their rural character. Smith would recognize much of Nomini Creek, for example. Lower tributary rivers like the St. Marys, Yeocomico, Coan, and Little Wicomico still retain a lovely, pastoral quality, but they too are growing.

A Treacherous Fish

Smith had spent an entire month exploring the Potomac, and he still wanted to check out the Rappahannock, the next major river south, before returning home. On their way back down the bay, he and his crew steered the *Discovery Barge* close along the eastern end of the Northern Neck. The map shows carefully noted detail for the Little and Great Wicomico Rivers, with Mosco's home village of Wighcocomoco marked with a King's House and the village of Cinquack with "Ordinary houses" at the mouth of today's Dividing Creek. He mapped Indian, Dymer, Tabbs, and Antipoison Creeks entering Fleets Bay, Windmill Point, and even Mosquito Creek just inside the Rappahannock's mouth. Chances are that the barge spent a night here before heading into the Rappahannock.

Smith must have been a master of persuasion. Though "our victual was near spent, he intended to see his imprisonment-acquaintances upon the river of Rapahannock, by many called Toppahanock." These would have been natives he met (and must have established friendly relations with) during his winter captivity, when Powhatan's warriors had paraded him from village to village. From that experience, he knew this river to be large enough to merit careful exploration, and he managed to persuade his crew to undertake it before heading back to Jamestown.

He steered for the south side of the Rappahannock's mouth but miscalculated the tide and ran the heavy barge hard aground on a shoal covered with underwater grass, with the water dropping. The crew "spied many fishes lurking in the reeds. Our captain, sporting himself—to catch them—by nailing them to the ground with his sword, set us all a-fishing in that manner; thus we took more in one hour than we could eat in a day."

If the fishmonger accompanying the crew offered Smith advice this time, the captain didn't take it. He speared a large, flat fish, "being much of the fashion of a thornback" (a European species of skate), but instead of a short tail with several knobs ("thorns"), this

Queen Anne's lace, opposite, blooms in late summer on the high portion of a marsh on the east side of the Nanticoke River just below and opposite the mouth of Marshyhope Creek. Over several centuries before and after Captain John Smith's time, this part of the river was home to a large, spread-out Nanticoke Indian town.

fish had a long, rounded tail "like a riding rod, whereon the middest is a most poisoned sting of two or three inches long, bearded [toothed] like a saw on each side, which she struck into the wrist of his arm near an inch and a half." A little blue spot appeared at the point of impact, but no blood.

Instead, Smith writhed instantly in excruciating pain. The fact that the *General History* describes the barb as being halfway down the tail marks the ray as a southern stingray, rather than a cownosed ray, the more prevalent species in the Chesapeake today, whose barb is set at the base of its tail. For either species, though, the barb is sharp, with reversed teeth that make it difficult to remove, and covered with a slime containing the poison that causes the pain.

As his arm swelled and the pain persisted, Smith directed the crew to dig his grave, but Dr. Walter Russell administered a "precious oil," and after four hours the pain began to subside. Smith took great satisfaction in eating part of his assailant "to his supper," then named the spot Stingray Ile, which survives today as Stingray Point, just east of Deltaville.

On this voyage, captain and crew probably spent the night nearby, possibly in the protected water of Fishing Bay, behind Stove Point Neck, just inside the mouth of the Piankatank, then headed back to Jamestown. But Smith was anxious to get right back on another Chesapeake voyage, to follow up on the places he had missed. Incredibly, within three days he was off again. During that long weekend the barge was repaired and re-outfitted, and Smith's health returned enough for him to plan another seven-week expedition. This one would have a trimmed-down crew of 12, plus the captain. Rejoining from the first expedition were nine toughened veterans. The only replacements were the tailor, the carpenter, a gentleman, and, interestingly, a different physician. The log during the stingray incident makes a point of mentioning that they had no surgeon, only a medical doctor. This time they were taking along Anthony Bagnall, the surgeon who attended Smith on his return. Perhaps the council agreed that the expedition would more likely need him than the colony.

On Sunday, July 24, 1608, the crew headed downriver again from Jamestown. The first expedition had journeyed nearly to the head of the bay and back, the men returning in reasonably good health. This second trip would not be so lucky.

Fog hovers over the James River at dawn, near the mouth of the Chickahominy. The Chesapeake's big rivers take on a ghostly appearance on mornings like this one.

Chapter Four

*I*n the discovery of this river some call Rapahanock
(…an excellent, pleasant, well inhabited, fertile,
and a goodly navigable river), we were kindly
entertained by the people of Moraughtacund.

— CAPTAIN JOHN SMITH,
General History, Book 3, Chapter 6

Reedgrass stands tall against a sunset on the Rappahannock. John Smith did not see much of this plant. It is native, but an aggressive strain from the Middle East has spread broadly around the bay in the past 50 years.

PRECEDING PAGES: Late afternoon light colors the Rappahannock River just above the bridge between the historic villages of Port Royal and Port Conway. The Discovery Barge crew came through here in August 1608, on the way back to Jamestown from the falls of the Susquehanna.

To the Head of the Bay and Back

On the second trip up the Chesapeake three days later, weather held Smith and the barge crew at Kecoughtan for a couple of days. The natives there believed that Smith was on his way to fight their mortal enemies, the Massawomeke, so they entertained them royally. When the wind turned fair (southerly), they sailed all the way up the bay in three days.

At the mouth of the Sassafras, they saw the bay divide into "two heads" and then into four. Moving clockwise from the west, these were the mouths of today's Susquehanna, Northeast, Elk, and Sassafras Rivers. They "searched far as we could sail them." In the process, they placed crosses at Peregryns Mount, a tall hill in the vicinity of present-day Elkton, Maryland, at the head of the Elk River; Gunters Harbour at the head of the Northeast River at the site of today's North East, Maryland; and just above "Smyths fales," the fall line of the "Sasquesahanough flue," apparently just above the site of today's Conowingo Dam on the south (Harford County) side. (Consistency of spelling, capitalization, and punctuation appears not to have been a priority for Smith, Todkill, and the other logkeepers.) Then they steered for the fourth "head," the Sassafras, although they did not yet know that the natives who lived on it called it Tockwogh.

In crossing from the Susquehanna to the Sassafras, however, they encountered seven or eight canoes of the Massawomeke. Two paddled out, unarmed, while the others "followed to second them if need required." Smith gave each of them a bell, which delighted the whole group so much that all came out to the barge, offering the captain "venison, bear's flesh, fish, bows, arrows, clubs, targets [shields], and bear's skins." Using sign language, they explained that they had just done battle with the Tockwogh people, who lived up the Tockwogh River. As evening fell, the two parties made a date to meet the next morning, but "after that we never saw them." Two pages later however, the *General History* notes that the Massawomeke went up a rocky river that Smith named Willowbye's Flue (now the Bush River), after the town he was born in and its lord of the manor.

Smith and his crew entered the Tockwogh, carrying all of the gifts from the Massawomeke. When the Tockwogh people saw the targets, bows, and arrows of the Massawomeke warriors, they jumped to the conclusion that the English had defeated those mortal enemies who had just attacked them, so they led the newly appointed heroes to their fortified town up the river for feasting, singing, and dancing. In the town, Smith and crew noticed hatchets, knives, and other metal tools that the Tockwogh said they had acquired in trade with the Susquehannock, "a mighty people and mortal enemies of the Massawomeke."

Smith observed, "The Sasquesahanocks inhabit upon the chief spring of these four branches of the bay's head, two days' journey higher than our barge could pass for rocks [at the falls]. Yet we prevailed with the interpreter to take with him another interpreter [fluent in the Susquehannock language] to persuade the Sasquesahanocks to come visit us…. Three or four days we expected [awaited] their return."

Some John Smith scholars believe that Smith and crew spent this time on present-day Garrett Island, the first island going up the Susquehanna. It is the largest of the lower river's islands and the only one that lies below Smith's Falls (as they are still known today), so it would have been easily accessible to the *Discovery Barge*. The island was an active volcano some 500 million years ago, and it retains a 100-foot-high summit of basaltic rock that would have provided an excellent lookout both upriver and down. Moreover, it would have provided sheltered access under any wind condition. These attributes may well have made it the customary neutral meeting place for the Susquehannock to trade with the Tockwogh.

Then "sixty of those giant-like people came down with presents of venison, tobacco pipes three foot in length, baskets, targets [shields], bows, and arrows." Smith was so impressed with the size of these Susquehannock chiefs and warriors that he placed an image of the chief prominently in the top right corner of his 1612 map, with the inscription "The Sasquesahanougs are a Gyant-like people & thus atyred." Since early 17th-century Englishmen averaged only 5 feet 4 inches in height, the Susquehannock must indeed have seemed like giants, but modern

This inset from Smith's 1612 map, opposite, shows the well-muscled, "gyant-like" Susquehannock chief that Smith met with at the mouth of the Susquehanna River. Archaeologists excavating the site of the Susquehannock town at present-day Washingtonboro, Pennsylvania find that these men averaged 5 feet 11 inches in height, moderate by today's standard but well above the 5-foot-4-inch average for Englishmen of the period.

The Sasques=ahanougs
are a Gyant like peo=ple &
Utchowig thus a tyred

SASQVE

FALL

In fall, summer's richness reaches a crescendo. Most of the bay's creatures—plants and animals alike—reach their physical peak for the year. Saltmarsh cordgrass down the bay and wild rice up the rivers fairly burst with green growth from the intense summer sun. All of that energy now goes into production of heavy seed heads. Along the riverbanks, the leaves of hardwood trees such as sycamores, red maples, and black gums begin to offer a brilliant mixture of yellow, orange, scarlet, and purple. On the Chickahominy, Pamunkey, Piankatank, and Pocomoke Rivers, the bald cypress trees turn rich hues of russet heather.

It's time to harvest all the growth of summer, whether that is seeds or soft-shell clams or fat young menhaden. Ironically, all of this bounty signals that it is time to prepare for winter. As the length of daylight gradually declines and the first cold fronts sweep in from the northwest, fish and birds sense the change of season. Ospreys that have taught their young to fly and fish now depart for Central and South America. Meanwhile, the first Canada geese sail in from their nesting grounds on Quebec's Ungava Peninsula.

At this season, predator fish gorge on large schools of baitfish. The most obvious are the small- to medium-size bluefish that harass young "peanut" menhaden as they school up in preparation to migrate out of the Chesapeake for the winter. They drive the baitfish to the surface, attacking as packs. Gulls sense the carnage and join in, diving on schools that are now threatened from above as well as below. Larger blues, gray trout, and rockfish often hang below, picking off scraps floating down without expending as much energy as the primary attackers. Some rock and most speckled trout quietly but effectively forage around points and marsh banks and holes in creeks and rivers. As the season progresses, mature female crabs head for the lower bay, carrying fertilized and developing eggs that they will lay the following spring.

A powerful whitetail buck browses along the edge of a wooded swamp on aptly named Deer Creek, just off the Susquehanna near Havre de Grace, Maryland.
DETAIL: *The head of a deer from the French soldier's engraving on page 70.*

archaeologists working around their village sites in Lancaster County, Pennsylvania, have found that the average height of Susquehannock men was 5 feet 11 inches, which seems only average to us in the early 21st century.

Smith's *General History* does not say much about this conversation with the Susquehannock, wherever it took place, but it appears to have been friendly. Upon its conclusion, five of the werowances climbed into the *Discovery Barge* for the ride to the Tockwogh village, since the wind across the Susquehanna Flats was too high for their own canoes.

They also told Smith and the barge crew a great deal about other Indian tribes, including those on the northern seaside of the Delmarva Peninsula and others on the Great Water and River of Canada beyond the mountains (the Great Lakes and the St. Lawrence River), with whom they traded for French hatchets and other tools. From this conversation, one thing was clear: The Susquehanna's rocks continued upstream, rendering it unfit for navigation by even a vessel as small as the *Discovery Barge*, much less for oceangoing sailing ships.

With this information, and the realization that Smith's Falls shut off any prospect of a Northwest Passage from the Chesapeake through North America, Smith and the crew bade the Tockwogh and Susquehannock farewell. Then, "having sought all the inlets and rivers worth noting" on this second voyage, they sailed quickly down the Chesapeake "to discover the River of *Pawtuxunt* [Patuxent]." Although Smith certainly had more waters to explore and map, he must have turned south with a certain sense of disappointment. He had now explored all three of the Chesapeake's largest rivers, the Susquehanna, the Potomac, and the James. He would now have to report to the Virginia Company of London that the Chesapeake offered no route to the Orient.

THE HISTORICAL SIGNIFICANCE OF SMITH'S VOYAGES

*T*oday the upper bay is a much altered place. Judging by his map, Smith hardly noticed the Back and Middle Rivers, but they are today part of a slow but steady renaissance on the east side of Baltimore County. Some of the Chesapeake's most skillful charter fishing skippers and watermen work out of the Middle River and adjacent Seneca Creek. There is also a rich heritage of waterfowl hunting and decoy carving here.

The next river, the Gunpowder, shows more detail on Smith's map, including some rocky areas indicative of its larger watershed and heavier flow. The lower part of this river, lying just inside Smith's "Powels Isles" (now Pooles Island), was navigable for shipping, giving rise to the port town of Joppa. From the mid-17th century until the mid-19th, Joppa flourished, but as farmers cleared land and began to plow up the Gunpowder watershed, heavy sediment flows silted in the harbor. Later in that century, the onset of a hundred years of gravel mining exacerbated the problem, as did suburban development in the second half of the 20th century. Today the anchorage that hosted schooners is a maze of shallow channels between marshy islands. It is a great place for bird-watchers and a good one for students on Chesapeake Bay Foundation canoe field trips to explore, but it is a difficult area for any larger vessel to navigate, even including outboard skiffs.

An old wooden "deadrise" workboat, opposite, lies abandoned along the shore of the Patuxent River near Broomes Island, Maryland. From the hull's lines, it's a reasonable guess that the boat was built nearby of local wood to catch river oysters with shaft tongs in the fall and winter and blue crabs with a trotline in the spring and summer.

FOLLOWING PAGES: Snow covers ice along the edges of the Gunpowder River near its falls, 20 miles north of Baltimore. Smith mapped the lower portion of this river, where Joppa became an important port in the 18th century.

Willowbye's Flue (the Bush River) has suffered the same fate. Headwater streams like Otter Point Creek are choked with sand, and open waters are filled with soft silt. Both sides of the lower Bush River belong to the U.S. Army's Aberdeen Proving Grounds, so access by recreational boats is restricted at times, and that part of the river is always patrolled by armed APG vessels.

The Susquehanna Flats have been central to the Chesapeake's history since Smith's time. Channels around the edges provide shipping access to Havre de Grace on the west side of the Susquehanna River's mouth and Perryville on the east (Cecil County) side, as well as to the town of North East. Before railroads, Havre de Grace was particularly valuable for shipping because the canal system from central Pennsylvania ended there. All three of these river towns have evolved from commercial fishing hubs for American shad and rockfish to recreational boating centers. Even so, all three retain strong local character. Havre de Grace and North East have worked particularly hard to preserve the waterfowl culture that began in the 17th century.

A water lily blooms in a marsh on the Potomac.

OPPOSITE PAGE:
Snow geese fly in silhouette in front of an almost-new moon. For centuries, the Chesapeake's wetlands and underwater grass meadows have attracted wintering waterfowl that have nested in summer in Canada.

The heart of this waterfowl culture was the flats, the habitat that lured migratory waterfowl such as scaup and canvasback ducks to migrate from nesting grounds in the potholes and sloughs of the Canadian prairies to winter on the Chesapeake. The allure was the food available on the flats, especially underwater grasses such as wild celery and sago pondweed, which grew in dense beds of hundreds of acres in the area. Overharvest of ducks and pollution from excess nitrogen, phosphorus, and sediment have greatly damaged the beds. Water quality improvements up the Susquehanna in Pennsylvania are slowly allowing the grasses and a few ducks to return, but reducing runoff pollution in this massive river's watershed remains a major challenge.

In spring, as the waterfowl depart, the Susquehanna Flats and the deep water immediately to the south attract large numbers of spawning rockfish. Although all of the Chesapeake's large rivers and many smaller ones host spawning rock each spring, this is the largest concentration not only in the bay but along the entire Atlantic coast. The Maryland Department of Natural Resources closes the spawning area to all harvest, commercial and recreational alike, during the season, though it does allow a catch-and-release sport fishery in the staging area on the flats themselves.

On the east side of the Susquehanna Flats, Elk Neck extends south to Turkey Point, a tall ridge that separates the flats from the Elk River.

Like the Gunpowder, the Elk River has suffered heavy sediment pollution over the past four centuries from agriculture and now suburban development, but its health and underwater grass beds are slowly improving.

One feature of the Elk is the Bohemia River, a pretty tributary that in the late 17th century was home to Augustine Herrman, a Bohemian nobleman who published the first real successor to John Smith's map in 1673. While Smith's map reflected the Chesapeake as it was at the time of the first sustained European contact, Herrman's map already showed Maryland and Virginia divided into counties with English names and marked with towns.

The Sassafras, too, was settled by Herrman's time, with the Tockwogh crowded out and assimilated into some larger tribe elsewhere. Sassafras Town, at the then-head of navigation, also silted in, so its English settlers moved downstream to the twin villages of Georgetown and Fredericktown, on the south and north sides of the river, respectively. The lower Sassafras remains a lovely, mostly wooded river, very popular as an anchorage for both cruising and day trip boaters. Its usually calm fresh waters make it especially inviting for swimming. As with

most upper Chesapeake waters, however, its primary problem is its proximity to Philadelphia and Wilmington and Newark, Delaware, from which many people descend on summer weekends.

THE PATUXENT

From the Sassafras, Smith's map indicates that he noted the bay's shoreline with reasonable care down to the mouth of the Chester, but then he sent the *Discovery Barge* on a beeline down past the "Rickards [Calvert] cliffes" to the Patuxent.

According to the map, it appears that Smith and crew followed the Eastern Shore down to today's Rock Hall harbor, in the process possibly meeting with the Ozinie tribe at their village (though he could also have included the village based on a map drawn by one of the Tockwogh). Then, however, he dismissed the next 50 miles of the Eastern Shore as covered by the Winstons Iles (today's Kent, Poplar, and Sharps Islands). Perhaps in their haste to get down the bay they got a good, long ride from a simultaneously fair wind and tide. It would, in any case, have taken them two days to make the 90-mile trip down to the mouth of the Patuxent.

Smith's text dismisses the Patuxent in a paragraph, but his map shows that he took pains to lay out the river's course and its native villages during a careful exploration. As usual, his measures of distance are inaccurate, but he got the shapes of the river's curves so exactly that it is easy to reconstruct his trip today. Two key landmarks are the werowance village of Pawtuxint on the river at the mouth of today's Battle Creek on the east side, and the lesser village Mattapanient, at the base of the large marsh on the west side that is now the Merkle Wildlife Management Area of the Maryland Department of Natural Resources.

Reconstructing the *Discovery Barge*'s trip up the Patuxent and back down is speculation, but there are several enduring realities of the river that give us some foundation for conjectures. The river is powerful: It is the longest river entirely within the borders of the state of Maryland. The headwaters lie on the Piedmont Plateau between Washington and Baltimore, squeezed between those of the Patapsco and the Anacostia. Most of the Patuxent's upper reaches, however, parallel the bay shoreline. For 40 miles, the river's floodplain runs due south from Bowie, Maryland, about 15 miles west of Annapolis.

In Smith's time, the Patuxent met the tide at Queen Anne's Bridge, about 15 miles above the site of Mattapanient. Below there,

As the sun rises, an early morning fog, opposite, burns off Lyons Creek, near where Captain John Smith placed one of his brass crosses at the upper point of his exploration of the Patuxent River.

Spawning carp churn the water in a cove on the Patuxent. These fish came to the Chesapeake and many other American waterways much later than the Jamestown colonists. Fishery biologists brought them here from Germany in the late 19th century under the mistaken assumption that the fish would be popular as food. Instead, they are widely considered to be nuisances, though a few people enjoy catching and eating them on bay rivers, including the Patuxent.

OPPOSITE PAGE:

An Indian couple shares a meal (possibly roasted chestnuts) in a watercolor by John White.

it flows narrow and deep, with powerful currents, through large meanders until it widens out below Benedict and curves southeast above Pawtuxunt. The reach below that curve runs 15 miles until the river turns east around today's Point Patience and out to the Chesapeake's main stem.

Throughout this course, the Patuxent flows through a number of narrow spots, beginning with the slot between Point Patience and California, where the channel is more than 100 feet deep. For the *Discovery Barge* crew, the ebb and flood currents in these places were both powerful friends and enemies, depending on which way they were headed. Meanwhile, the curves would have caused the winds to shift back and forth, making sailing difficult, especially as the river narrowed. They would have had to play the tides carefully and row considerable distances.

The map indicates that they probably began their Patuxent exploration at the village of Opanient, on the east side just below the mouth of present-day St. Leonard's Creek. The people here would have been fishermen, depending on the river's abundant oyster reefs and fish, including spring runs of shad, herring, rockfish, and sturgeon as well as summer visitors such as Atlantic croakers, Norfolk spot, and sheepshead. It is a reasonable guess that Smith stopped to make friends, inquire where the werowance lived, and ask for information about the course of the river. It is also possible that he took a native guide aboard as a pilot. The barge would then have made its way to Pawtuxunt, where the "tractable and civil" werowance and his people would have feasted the captain and crew.

In all, Smith mapped eight native villages on each side of the Patuxent, including Acquaskack, which survives today as the rural hamlet of Aquasco on the west side, and Mattapanient, whose name survives as Mattaponi Creek, also on the west side between the Merkle Wildlife Management Area and the Patuxent River Park. The upper villages would have had easy access to the river's "breadbasket marshes" of wild rice, arrow arum, and arrowhead.

Anyone who prowls the Patuxent today will find that the historical traditions have endured. The Patuxent River Park, operated by the Maryland National Capital Park and Planning Commission, has preserved several thousand acres of riverfront between Magruder's Landing and Queen Anne's Bridge. Across the river on the east side, the Jug Bay Wetlands Sanctuary does the same. Battle Creek Cypress Swamp, at the head of the creek above the site of Pawtuxunt, preserves one of the northernmost natural stands of bald cypress trees. At the mouth of the river, the town of Solomons is home to both the Calvert Marine Museum and the Chesapeake Biological Laboratory of the University of Maryland.

It is remarkably easy today to find "John Smith views" on the Patuxent, especially since parts of the river like Mattaponi Creek are less than 25 miles from Washington, D.C.'s Capitol Hill. The broad marshes and their creeks remain a delight to the eye, a magnet for wintering waterfowl, and keystone communities for the Patuxent's largemouth bass, white perch, catfish, great blue herons, ospreys, and bald eagles.

However, the river has had to endure endless ecological insults, especially in the past 50 years. Its 400 years of tobacco agriculture began

ROCKFISH

 The striped bass is the Chesapeake's best-loved fish, a high distinction in such a splendid aquatic community. Fully three-quarters of the Atlantic coastal stock hatch in spring in the upper tidal reaches of the bay's large and medium-size rivers, waters with currents strong enough to keep their eggs suspended through their first weeks of life. Those that escape from herons, river otters, and even larger members of their species grow up to five inches on the abundance of their first Chesapeake summer. By fall, these aggressive little eating machines will even attack anglers' lures nearly their own size.

Over the next several years, these "puppy" rockfish will become "schoolies," hanging out with others of the same size, terrorizing small baitfish such as silversides and bay anchovies, prowling underwater grass beds in search of crabs. They'll winter in the Chesapeake's deepwater sanctuaries where temperatures are stable (specific heat again) but otherwise haunt both open waters and shallow creeks. By the time they reach 25 inches in length, most will begin migrating out into the Atlantic and up the coast, to spend the summer foraging as far north as the Bay of Fundy, though most will stay in the waters of southern New England.

In the fall, they begin to feed heavily. It is now that bay anglers delight in fishing for the rock that have stayed here. On Indian summer mornings and evenings, the fish prowl some of the Chesapeake's most interesting places, from lonely marsh guts around Tangier Sound, where John Smith and his crew dodged thunder squalls, to restored oyster reefs in Norfolk's Elizabeth and Lafayette Rivers, where Smith and his crew found no one but which are now part of a sprawling metropolis. Later in the fall, the large rock that have spent the summer north will reappear to feed on all of the menhaden, spot, trout, and other fish heading out to the Atlantic for the winter.

A yearling rockfish (striped bass) prowls through an eelgrass bed in the lower Chesapeake. The bay and its rivers are both cradle and nursery for about 75 percent of the rockfish of the Atlantic coast.
DETAIL: *A fish (possibly a large white perch), taken from a 16th-century engraving.*

the process of sedimentation, but heavy residential, commercial, and highway development in the Baltimore-Washington corridor have loaded it unmercifully with nitrogen and phosphorus pollution from poorly treated sewage, sediment, and urban-suburban runoff. Sedimentation has been heavy enough that the head of navigation has moved downriver seven miles, from Queen Anne's Bridge to just above Wayson's Corner.

THE RAPPAHANNOCK

*S*mith remained determined to explore the Rappahannock, so after mapping the Patuxent, he made for Windmill Point, on the north side of its mouth, turned the corner, and headed up that "excellent, pleasant, well inhabited, fertile, and a goodly navigable river."

The map shows a chief's house at Cuttatawomen, in the vicinity of today's Kilmarnock, and five smaller villages between Mosquito Point and the Corrotoman River, but the first encounter came at the chief's house at Moraughtacund (today's Morattico), where they were

reunited with Mosco. He was just as kind and helpful as before, but he warned Smith not to cross the river, because, having accepted the hospitality of the Moraughtacund people, he would be considered an enemy by the Rapahannock tribe there. It seems that the Moraughtacund chief had recently "stol'n" three of the Rapahannock chief's wives.

Smith, however, ordered his crew to begin sailing the *Discovery Barge* upriver, although he did heed Mosco's advice to arrange the Massawomeck targets (shields), which the barge still carried, around the bow "like a forecastle." Sure enough, a dozen or so Rapahannocks appeared on the far shore at the mouth of a creek (possibly the Piscataway) with a good landing and trade goods in some canoes. They appeared friendly and readily agreed to exchange hostages.

Smith selected the stalwart Anas Todkill as the English hostage. Once ashore, that worthy, being just as pragmatic as his captain, asked to "go over the plain to fetch some wood," but his captors would not let him do so unless Smith brought the barge close to shore in the creek. Through this negotiation, Todkill managed to get "two stone's throws" toward the woods, where he saw several hundred warriors hiding in ambush. As he tried to return to the shore, they grabbed him and began to take him away. He called out to the barge that they were betrayed, at which cry the Rapahannock hostage jumped overboard to swim to shore. James Watkins, his keeper, killed him, and the barge crew fired a volley into the woods.

In the confusion, Todkill escaped his captors, but they shot so many arrows so quickly that he fell to the ground and hid. After the warriors shot "more than a thousand arrows," they turned and retreated into the woods. Smith and crew now went ashore with the shields and rescued Todkill, who was smeared with Rapahannock blood but "had no hurt."

The English "heard no more of them," so they began to break the arrows, but they saved an armful for Mosco, and awarded him the Rapahannock canoes as well. These were precious commodities, since it took a man a full day to make a single arrow and canoes much more time, so Mosco was delighted. Then they returned to Moraughtacund to rig the barge all around with the Massawomeck shields.

The next morning, they headed upriver again, with Mosco first running along the shore and then climbing into the boat. As the barge passed the villages of Pisacack, Matchopeak, and Mecuppom on the 150-foot-high Fones Cliffs, the Rapahannocks ambushed them again, having hidden themselves behind small bushes at the edge of today's Paynes Island marsh on the other side. The arrows, however, struck the shields

PAGES 124-125:
Wind-driven ripples have formed on this long beach that stretches from Winter Harbor to Hole in the Wall, between Mobjack Bay and the mouth of the Piankatank on the bay's lower western shore.

Trees and shrubs, opposite, grow right to the edge of deep water on the Rappahannock's Occupacia Creek.

Cypress trees, below, grow out into a tidal fresh marsh in the delta where Dragon Run flows into the head of the Piankatank River. The beautiful run drains Dragon Swamp, which forms the county line between Gloucester and Mathews to the south and Essex and Middlesex to the north.

OPPOSITE PAGE:

A great blue heron watches a fish, assessing its chances for a catch in a Chesapeake creek. Though they nest in raucous colonial rookeries (see p. 60), these expert fishermen lead mostly solitary lives for the rest of the year.

and fell harmlessly into the river. Smith again ordered a volley of shot, which dispersed them. They reappeared on the shore later, "dancing and singling very merrily."

Smith, writing from memory 16 years later, abruptly shifts his narrative to note that the kings of Pissaseck (today's Leedstown, just upriver from Fones Cliffs), Nantaughtacund (further upriver in today's Portobago Bay), and Cuttatawomen (another king's house on the river's tight curve to the north several miles above the old town of Port Royal) "used us kindly" and welcomed Mosco with them.

Now, just above Cuttatawomen, between Secobeck (Skinkers Neck) and Massawteck (Moss Neck), the barge saw its only fatality in the 1608 summer cruises. Richard Featherstone, a veteran of the first voyage, died aboard of an unspecified malady. In the *General History,* Smith remembered that he "had behaved himself honestly, valiantly, and industriously" during his time in Virginia. They buried him with a volley of shot in the river at "Fetherstone's [sic] Bay," possibly at the mouth of a little marshy creek on Moss Neck. Smith notes that in spite of all the hardships they endured, the rest of the crew "had all well recovered their healths."

The next day, they made their way up to the Rappahannock's fall line (today's Fredericksburg), where they went ashore, planting two brass crosses and looking for "stones, herbs, and springs," without seeing any natives. After an hour, however, their sentry saw an arrow fall near him. Suddenly, there were "an hundred nimble Indians skipping from

tree to tree, letting fly their arrows as fast as they could." The English too used the trees to hide themselves while they returned fire, but Mosco was the one who turned the tide. He shot arrows back, which confused the attackers, and made enough noise as he moved around that they thought he was "many." After half an hour, they retreated.

Returning to the barge, they found a wounded native, "which Mosco seeing, never was dog more furious against a bear than Mosco was to have beat out his brains." Smith restrained him, however, so that surgeon Anthony Bagnall dressed the wound. Soon, the patient recovered enough to "eat and speak," while Smith mollified Mosco by helping him gather up more arrows.

At Smith's request, Mosco questioned the man, who gave his name as Amoroleck and his tribe as Hassinunga, well upriver toward the mountains, at the fork where today's Rapidan River enters the Rappahannock (according to Smith's map). They were accompanied also by the neighboring kings of Stegora, Tauxuntania, and Shakahonea. He said that he and his mates had come to nearby Mohaskahod, a fishing/hunting camp, and attacked because they had heard that the English had "come from

under the world to take their world from them" (an assessment that would in the next hundred years prove all too true). Mosco questioned him about what lay beyond the mountains. He did not know but did give them some information about the Monacan and Massawomeke tribes. He also said that he was a brother to the Hassinunga chief.

Waiting till dark, with the Massawomeke shields set on the barge, Smith, the crew, Mosco, and Amoroleck began quietly to row down the narrow river. Sure enough, Hassinunga arrows began hitting the targets and dropping into the river. The warriors made so much noise that they could not hear Amoroleck yelling to them that he was being treated well. Finally, at dawn, Smith anchored the barge and the crew ate breakfast. "Being well refreshed," they armed themselves with the shields on their arms, took up their swords, and showed themselves to the Hassinunga. Amoroleck told them that the English were friendly, that Mosco, the Patawomeck, loved them dearly, and that they had prevented him from killing Amoroleck.

The warriors hung their bows in trees, laid down their arrows, and presented Smith with a bow and a full quiver. Then the four kings met with Smith and crew on shore to talk and trade. The English were amused to find that the warriors thought their pistols were ornate smoking pipes. Then they left "four or five hundred of our merry Mannahocks [apparently another name for the Hassinunga] and set sail for Moraughtacund."

The Moraughtacund people rejoiced that the English had made peace with the Mannahock chiefs, who had previously fought with them. Now they wanted Smith to make peace with the Rapahannock chief as well. He replied that because they had "twice assaulted him that came only in love to do them good," he would revenge himself unless they "made satisfaction," including meeting with him unarmed, presenting the chief's bow and arrows, becoming friends with the Moraughtacund people, and giving him the chief's only son in pledge of friendship. They sent to Rapahannock, asking to meet "where they first fought" (at LaGrange, Piscataway, or Hoskins Creek), as well as to the Nantaughtacund and Pissaseck chiefs.

All appeared at the appointed place and hour, and Rapahannock complied with all the demands except for his son, whom he declared he could not live without. Instead, he offered Smith the three women that Moraughtacund had stolen. (Apparently the women had no say in the matter.) Smith accepted the offer, and everyone piled into the assembled boats to cross to Moraughtacund.

Fall colors, opposite, glow with afternoon sunlight on the Rappahannock's Totuskey Creek. The rolling topography of the land on both sides of this large tidal river drains rainwater into long, deep creeks that remain largely as they were when the Moraughtacund and Rapahannock peoples lived along them.

FOLLOWING PAGES: A wooden bridge connects a path between two marshes at the Chesapeake Bay Foundation's Port Isobel Island Environmental Education Center near Tangier, Virginia. Here students and many of the region's decision-makers come to study the Chesapeake in its most natural state near the place where John Smith and the Discovery Barge crew endured their first Chesapeake thunderstorm.

Here Smith had to work out a tricky problem. He had no need of a wife—indeed, he never married, and there is no record of any relationship he had with a woman—but he did not want to offend Rapahannock. He gave each woman a beaded necklace, then asked Rapahannock to take "the one he loved best." The next choice went to Moraughtacund, and the third to Mosco.

There began several days of feasting and dancing, with "not a bow nor arrow seen amongst them." Mosco changed his name to *uttasantasough,* or "stranger," the same name the natives used for the English, declaring his kinship with them. All the natives swore friendship with the English, promising to plant corn for them the next year, and Smith promised trade goods. Then the barge departed, amid loud goodbyes and a ceremonial volley of shot.

Smith and his crew made their way around Stingray Point to the Piankatank and anchored in it for the night, possibly in Fishing Bay or farther upriver around the mouth of today's Healy's Creek. The next day, they "discovered it so high as it was navigable," probably at the point where it shoals up in the delta of Dragon Run, the long bottomland swamp creek that forms its headwater, about 18 miles above the mouth. They found women, children, and a few old men tending corn, which the natives offered to the English. Apparently all of the younger men were out hunting. After mapping this relatively short river, Smith directed the *Discovery Barge* out into the Chesapeake to head back toward Jamestown.

MODERN PARADOXES

*T*oday, the Rappahannock and the Piankatank are paradoxes. The shorelines of both are relatively unspoiled. True, they are hardly wilderness, but for the most part, their houses are interspersed with wooded shorelines. On both, the farther one goes upriver, the fewer houses there are. As commercial fishing and oystering have declined over the past 40 years, though, both lower rivers have become much more the province of recreational boaters. On the Piankatank, Gwynns Island at the mouth on the south side bustles in season with summer people and all year with watermen and the U.S. Coast Guard's Milford Haven Station.

As one goes up the Rappahannock, the houses become farther apart. Smith's village of Moraughtacund, now Morattico, still has a distinctly rural feel, with much of its economy still based on crabbing, though its formerly rich oyster stocks declined precipitously in the 1980s and '90s. Tappahannock is a bustling market crossroad, but it still has a small-town feel. Across from it is the large Island Farm Marsh, still full of muskrat houses.

Above there, much of the Rappahannock looks the way Captain John Smith and his crew saw it, especially around Fones Cliffs and Horsehead Cliffs, about eight miles upriver. Both are major eagle roosts, with several hundred birds from the mid-Atlantic and Northeast spending the winter there. Meanwhile, the marshes are home to thousands of wintering waterfowl. The shorelines here mix woodlands with marshes and large farms, many of them in the same family for a century or more. Willing landowners have now preserved a number of those farms and the varied habitats they offer by selling them or donating conservation easements on them to the Rappahannock River Valley National Wildlife Refuge.

It is no accident that Smith mapped many native villages in this part of the river. From Fones Cliffs upstream, the marshes on

A mature bald eagle, opposite, takes flight from a tree on the edge of Fones Cliffs on the Rappahannock River. These cliffs, where Rapahannock warriors ambushed the Discovery Barge, *and Horsehead Cliffs ten miles upstream form the core of a major eagle roost that sometimes holds more than 300 birds.*

the main river and in large, powerful creeks like Cat Point and Occupacia still grow all of the staple "breadbasket" food plants the natives depended on to supplement their corn crops. The same goes for the upper Piankatank.

The paradox is that while both of these rivers appear to be unspoiled, both are badly unbalanced by nitrogen, phosphorus, and sediment. Both rivers run too cloudy for the consistent and extensive underwater grass beds that their fish, crabs, and waterfowl used to enjoy, and both have had recurring algae-fueled "dead zones" of depleted dissolved oxygen in recent years.

THE END OF THE VOYAGE

The day was calm, and the bay flat ("deesh ca'm," or dish calm, as watermen called it 50 years ago). The crew rowed toward Point Comfort, but when night fell, they dropped anchor in Gosnold's Bay (today's Poquoson Flats, at the mouth of the river of the same name). Here another thunder squall ambushed them. Bailing as quickly as they could, they weighed anchor, set the sails, and ran before the wind, making their way by the lightning flashes all the way to Point Comfort.

Today, the Poquoson River benefits from only minimal runoff, though many of its coves are heavily developed by the fast-growing suburban communities of York County and the incorporated City of Poquoson. Its waters remain clear enough to sustain large eelgrass beds on the flats, while the nearby Big Salt Marsh offers additional habitat for abundant fish, crabs, and water birds. The marsh is in fact the largest on the western shore of the bay, but it offers a paradox. Exploring a waterway deep in the marsh like Sandy Bay by canoe or kayak places the modern explorer deep in one of the most productive communities of the Chesapeake ecosystem, but looking above the marsh to the skyline reveals a close view of the lunar lander at the nearby Langley NASA Center. Fortunately, the Big Marsh is protected as part of the Plumtree Island National Wildlife Refuge.

There's a great irony here. What really protects the southern section of the marsh is a collection of unexploded bombs dropped over the years in training exercises by pilots from Langley Air Force Base. The U.S. Fish and Wildlife Service keeps people out of the refuge for their own safety, though their efforts certainly help to keep the Big Marsh close to the condition of the marsh that Smith and his crew passed as they fled the thunderstorm on the way to Point Comfort.

For lesser men, that harrowing "adventure" would have been enough reason to return home as soon as possible, but this crew was different, as the *General History* describes in Book 3, Chapter 6: "There refreshing ourselves, because we had only but heard of the Chisapeacks and Nandsamunds we thought it as fit to know all our neighbors near home as so many nations abroad. So setting sail for the southern shore, we sailed up a narrow river up the country of Chisapeack."

This narrow river was today's Elizabeth, the four-branched, urban waterway that divides Norfolk from Portsmouth and contains the headquarters of the U.S. Navy's Atlantic Fleet. The year before the *Discovery Barge*'s visit, Powhatan had attacked and killed most of the Chesapeake tribe, for whom, ironically, the great bay would be named. Historians believe that the nearby Nansemond absorbed whatever remnant of the tribe survived. Smith mapped their river quickly, noting "a good channel" but a narrow course, a scattering of houses

and gardens, and "the greatest pine and fir trees we ever saw in the country," but no people.

Smith would see plenty of people on the Elizabeth today. It is an urban river with hardened working shorelines, dredged channels, toxic sediments, industrial and sewage wastewater discharges, large ships, and a human population over a million. Amazingly, it still retains a few attractive residential neighborhoods, especially on its tributary Lafayette River and Western Branch. Restoration oyster reefs, built by the Virginia Marine Resources Commission and planted by the Chesapeake Bay Foundation's staff and local volunteers, have brought at least some "live bottom" to the river, while the Elizabeth River Project, a partnership between business and the community, has carried out important cleanup projects. The Elizabeth is still one of the three most polluted tributaries of the bay (on that dubious list with Baltimore Harbor and the Anacostia River), but its fortunes are slowly improving as the people around it realize that a live river is more valuable than a sewer.

In a story Smith told in the 1624 *General History,* the barge returned to "the great river" (Hampton Roads) and headed west toward the Nansemond River, noting multiple oyster reefs. They saw several Nansemond fishermen tending weirs, but the natives fled at the sight of the barge. Smith went ashore to leave "divers toys" (small trade goods) and returned to the barge. Soon the Nansemond returned and beckoned them back, singing and dancing. One of them invited the crew to his house up the river and came aboard for the journey, while the others ran along shore. The fisherman led them "seven or eight miles" up the narrow river to an area full of cornfields. He told Smith that the rest of the tribe were away hunting and invited the crew into his house on a small island, where they gave more trinkets to him and his family.

Now the other fishermen paddled to the island and invited the crew farther up the river to see their houses. The river got narrower, though, and the natives went ashore to "fetch their bows and arrows" and would not go back out onto the water. "This gave us cause to provide for the worst," Smith and his logkeepers wrote.

Indeed, Smith and crew had learned well how to read the signals: "Far we went not ere seven or eight canoes full of men armed appeared following us." Arrows soon began flying from the riverbanks, as well as the canoes, "but amongst them we bestowed so many

A tiny creek, opposite, meanders through the salt marsh at Bishops Head, across Hooper Strait from Bloodsworth Island (Smith's Limbo). The large Bishops Head marsh is now part of the Blackwater National Wildlife Refuge, while its southern tip is home to the Chesapeake Bay Foundation's Karen Noonan Center for Environmental Education.

shot the most of them leaped overboard and swam ashore." The English muskets had greater range than the Nansemond bows, so the skirmish ended quickly.

The barge crew suffered no casualties beyond the fact that Anthony Bagnall had one arrow in his hat and another in his shirt-sleeve. The abandoned canoes floated free in the river. The barge crew collected them and moored them in open water. Smith and crew debated whether to call for a parley or burn the village outright. As they talked, they began to cut a couple of the canoes in pieces. Each of these boats represented weeks of hard work by Nansemond craftsmen. That act of destruction settled the issue quickly. The Nansemond warriors laid down their bows and asked for peace—and their boats.

Smith replied that his terms were their kings' bows and arrows, a "chain of pearl," and 400 baskets of corn on their next visit. The alternative was destruction of the villages, the corn, and the canoes. The Nansemond accepted these terms. "So much [corn] as we could carry we took. And so departing good friends, we returned to James Town, where we safely arrived the 7 of September, 1608." Thus ended the *Discovery Barge*'s two extraordinary voyages of exploration.

The present-day Nansemond, too, is quite different from what it was in Smith's time. While the city of Suffolk at its head of navigation claims the distinction of the second-highest vertical tide change in the Chesapeake system, at 1.0-4.9 feet, depending on the moon (second only to 3.2-5.1 feet at Walkerton, Virginia, on the Mattaponi), the river has been modified significantly for navigation and water supply, and the oyster reefs at its mouth are faint shadows of their former selves.

The headwaters are now impounded into three water-supply lakes, and while they offer great freshwater recreational fishing, the dams have flooded the breadbasket marshes of wild rice and arrow arum that sustained the Nansemond village. Meanwhile, spoil from channel dredging now covers the banks, growing reedgrass and big cordgrass, which, while they help to stabilize those banks, do not offer the wildlife values of their predecessors. For a view of what the mouth of the 17th-century Nansemond River might have looked like, the Candy Island salt marsh just upriver, preserved by the Virginia Department of Game and Inland Fisheries, is a better choice. Even so, the river's broad salt marshes still have "hammocks" of wooded high land that would have served well as island homes for the Nansemond in Smith's time.

Canada geese fly in front of an October hunter's moon rising over the Blackwater National Wildlife Refuge, near Cambridge on Maryland's Eastern Shore. Since the late 1930s, the refuge has preserved thousands of acres of prime Chesapeake marshes and wooded wetlands, while allowing controlled public access to some of its most interesting wildlife habitats.

Chapter Five

The 12 of January {1609}, we arrived at Werowocomoco, where the {York} river was frozen near half a mile from the shore. But ... the president with his barge so far had approached by breaking the ice ... rather than to lie there frozen to death, by his own example he taught them to march near middle deep ... through this muddy, frozen ooze."

— CAPTAIN JOHN SMITH,
General History, Book 3, Chapters 7-8

Above the village of Aylett, Virginia, the Mattaponi River disappears into a tunnel of trees. Even so, Aylett and Rosepout, just downstream, were minor colonial ports for shipping out timber from nearby woods and both tobacco and grain from surrounding farms.

PRECEDING PAGES: *The sun sets over the Chesapeake near Cape Charles.*

Working Rivers

*I*t is relatively easy to follow John Smith through the two exploratory voyages in the summer of 1608. Those voyages were certainly no picnic because of the heat, the hard work of rowing the *Discovery Barge,* the poor food and water, and the anxiety of dealing with unforeseen hazards, especially in meeting new tribes who might or might not be friendly. Even so, the day-to-day hazards and hardships of life in Virginia and dealing with the various natives on a continued basis were arguably just as difficult, especially on winter trips like the one to Werowocomoco described in this chapter's opening quotation. Smith's explorations of the James and York River systems were built not only on pure exploration but also the continual need to feed the colony. Thus he made 15 trips to various parts of the James and its two largest tributaries, the Chickahominy and the Appomattox, as well as six up the York (which the natives called "Pamunkee") and the two branches that form it, the Pamunkey and the Mattaponi.

A week after the First Landing, captains Newport and Smith and 20 others departed to explore the James River to the head of the tide. They must have taken the *Discovery Barge,* because of its shallow draft, and, because of the size of the group, another vessel, possibly the small *Discovery.* The winds both helped and hindered them, because the James above the mouth of the Appomattox becomes narrow and winds into ever tighter meanders. It took them six days to cover the 70-plus miles from Jamestown to the falls of the James and back.

On the way, they passed "divers small habitations," but just below the falls, they found "a town called Powhatan, consisting of some twelve houses pleasantly seated on a hill, before it three fertile isles, about it many of their cornfields." The "prince of this town," Smith says, "is called Powhatan [though he was actually Tanxpowhatan, son of the great chief], and his people the Powhatan," which name they also gave to the river.

The falls lay "within a mile" above the town. The "pleasant seat" would have been atop today's Marion Hill, at the east end of the city of Richmond, which grew up later as the port at the head of navigation on the James. Smith's map shows five of the other six hills upon which Richmond sits, with his cross placed up in the rapids, probably in the vicinity of today's Hollywood Cemetery.

A MAJOR RIVER
BUT NO NORTHWEST PASSAGE

*F*rom this point, the headwaters of the James extend westward for 300 miles, to the edge of the Alleghany Plateau in southwestern Virginia. Building on Smith's explorations and his map, European settlers moved west from the falls in the late 17th century, filling the valley with farms and villages that grew in time into cities such as Charlottesville (on the tributary Rivanna River), Lynchburg, and Covington (on the Jackson River). Since the advent of the moldboard plow (which Thomas Jefferson promoted on his estate near the Rivanna), the river has carried copious quantities of "red clay" from the Piedmont lands that drain to it.

Lynchburg and Richmond have contributed equally copious quantities of sewage and urban stormwater, some of it untreated, and Hopewell has added industrial wastewater, which led to the infamous kepone insecticide debacle of the mid-1970s. Meanwhile, overfishing has decimated the stock of sturgeon, American shad, and oysters, which have also suffered from pollution and disease.

Even so, life in the James persists, including a tiny young-of-the-year Atlantic sturgeon caught in 2004 in a trawl net near Hopewell by a Chesapeake Bay Foundation workboat with a class of middle school science students aboard. The federal Clean Water Act and more recent water quality standards promulgated by the Commonwealth of Virginia have significantly improved the river, though much more pollution reduction is necessary to restore the river to a semblance of health. The water is perpetually colored from suspended soil particles or algae blooms, but shad runs are rebuilding and many rockfish also spawn upriver in the spring. Powell's Creek on the south side (whose mouth Smith mapped opposite Weyanoke) boasts a major bald eagle roost, the epicenter of a strong population

Red maple leaves, opposite, collect in a tiny eddy in Herring Creek, off the James River, in the fall. The swirling material at the surface is actually foam from the natural breakdown of leaves and other detritus (formerly living material) that are natural parts of the creek's food web.

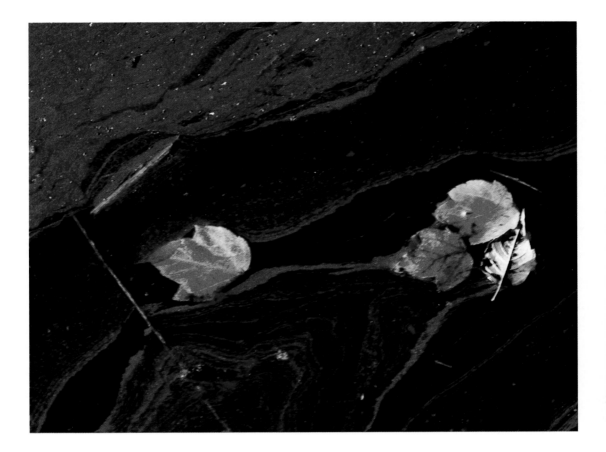

of the birds along the river. The abundant wild rice marshes upriver of Jamestown that fed Powhatan's people four centuries ago still attract large numbers of migratory waterfowl in fall and winter.

Upriver, two introduced fish species, largemouth bass and huge blue catfish, thrive while attracting anglers from near and far. Downriver, rockfish offer a strong fishery for saltwater anglers throughout most of the year. The owners of numerous historic sites along the river have grown increasingly adept at helping visitors understand how the natural history of the river has driven the development of both native and more recent culture along it, and how in turn we humans have affected the river.

The First Major Ambush

After visiting the falls, the English worked their way back down to Powhatan village, the mouth of the Appomattox River (where "the Queen…kindly entreated us"), and Weanock, where the natives were

"churlish." Newport had wanted to visit Paspahegh, on the north bank of the James just above the mouth of the Chickahominy, but with a fair wind, he decided to head straight for the fort.

That wind was a happy chance. The explorers had left with no palisades around the fort. In their absence, "400 Indians the day before had assaulted the fort and surprised it." The colonists were planting corn, with their arms stored away, except for several gentlemen who had their matchlock muskets with them. Cannon fire from their ships scared the attackers into retreat, but not before the Indians had wounded about 20 men and killed one of the boys of the colony. The attackers were presumably Paspahegh, on whose territory the English had set-tled without asking permission. "With all due speed we palisadoed our fort," Smith continues, and for the next week the threat of another ambush hung over them.

TRADING FOR CORN
ON THE CHICKAHOMINY

*C*aptain Newport left for England in early June. The colonists had enough provisions to last through the summer. Internal squabbles, mis-management of resources by the some of the gentlemen on the council, and disease affected everyone, including Smith. He recovered, as did about half of the men, but the other half died that summer.

In September, with only a few weeks of provisions left, some neighboring Paspahegh brought corn to the fort, but it was not enough to last long. Migratory waterfowl began to filter into the James and the Chickahominy (as they still do today) in such huge numbers that even the colonists' muskets proved accurate enough to bring them down.

Smith took the barge downriver to Kecoughtan to "try the river for fish." That late-season attempt was unsuccessful, though the colonists had lived well on sturgeon during the spring and summer. So was trading for corn, at least at first, but the captain turned out to be a skillful negotiator. Between Kecoughtan, Warrascoyack (near Smithfield on today's Pagan River), and Quiyoughcohannock (Claremont), Smith managed to find enough corn to keep the colony going into December.

As fall graded into winter, he made three successful trips up the Chickahominy, reaching well above today's Lanexa, where the city of Newport News erected a dam in 1938 to impound drinking water. Today those waters form Chickahominy Lake, but in 1607, they were tidal.

This particular view of the Appomattox River, opposite, looks down to its junction with the James, just above the present-day site of Hopewell, Virginia. The Queen of the Appa-mattuck tribe was cordial to the English colonists when they stopped to visit her during their first exploration of the James.

The natives of this river had maintained their independence from Powhatan and so tended to be friendlier than the Paspahegh, who were subject to him and still upset with the English.

A Rich River

*E*ven today, the Chickahominy is a jewel, though development around Williamsburg is quickly increasing pollution pressures on it. The river's long, swampy headwaters, which parallel Interstate 64 running east from Richmond, catch and filter the rainwater flowing into it, providing a valuable natural water-treatment system that results in clear water in the lower reaches, colored like iced tea from the tannins in leaves of wet-ground trees such as red maple, black gum, and green ash, and the needles of bald cypress. This river winds down to the James between broad rice marshes, still providing some of the finest natural vistas in the Chesapeake system, as well as good fishing and great bird-watching. Anyone who explores the Chickahominy today will have no trouble seeing why it was so valuable to the native Paspahegh and Chickahominy peoples.

MEETINGS WITH OPECHANCANOUGH
AND POWHATAN

*B*y late December, the supplies were nearly exhausted again, so Smith made one more trip up the Chickahominy, this time trying also to explore the headwaters of the river. By the time he got around where today's Route 155 crosses the river near Providence Forge, the river was narrow and full of fallen trees, several of which he cut his way through. (The barge must have been well stocked with tools.) Here he left the barge with instructions to the crew to stay on board.

Taking two men, he hired two natives and a canoe from the village of Apocant and headed upstream to go "a-fowling." Stopping ashore to eat, Smith decided to take one of his guides and continue by land. Soon, he ran afoul of a large hunting party led by Opechancanough, Powhatan's brother and eventual successor, who was then chief of the Pamunkey on the next river to the north, the main tributary of today's York. Wielding his matchlock pistol, Smith seized his guide as a hostage but slipped in the mud beside the river and fell. At that point, he "resolved to try their mercies." His guide informed the attackers that Smith was the leader of the expedition, which caused them to treat him with respect.

OPPOSITE PAGE:
Canada geese take off from the Turkey Island Bend in the James River, adjacent to the Presqu'ile National Wildlife Refuge above Hopewell. Once a long peninsula with the early colonial settlement of Bermuda Hundred at its base, Presqu'ile is now an island, with a channel cut through its base to shorten the run upriver to Richmond for shipping.

Pickerelweed, arrow arum, and arrowhead grow in a tidal fresh marsh on the Chickahominy River. The latter two produce starchy tubers that were staples in the diet of the Chickahominy people. The quality of these marshes, which also grow abundant wild rice, was a factor in the large number of Chickahominy living on the river. Smith mapped 14 villages there.

WINTER

In winter, the cold-blooded creatures of the Chesapeake slow down, because their body temperature and metabolism closely follow the water temperature. Those that can move seek out the warmest, most stable water they can find.

As is true in other seasons, water's high specific heat governs their behavior. The most stable water has the greatest volume, found in the deepest holes of the rivers and the open bay. Because water is densest at 4 degrees Celsius (39.2 degrees Fahrenheit), that is the temperature of the Chesapeake's deepest water in all but the mildest winters, while colder water floats over it. Because of this peculiar characteristic of water, blue crabs burrow in deep areas of mud and sand, while overwintering fish such as rock and white perch spend the winter in a near-dormant state in deep troughs, including the ancestral Susquehanna channel on the east side of the Chesapeake off Kent Island, the lower Potomac off Tall Timbers, and the trench off Smith Point Light.

Meanwhile, sessile (stationary) animals such as oysters and clams slow down their work of filtering bay water but continue to feed off the algae that bloom in the sunlight that gradually increases after the winter solstice, while barnacles continue to draw in food particles with their feather-like "legs." Marine worms and tiny crustacean scavengers such as amphipods, which have limited mobility, slowly work their way through the scraps of once-alive material that accumulate on the bay's bottom.

The most active bay animals are warm-blooded—birds, mammals, and humans who eke out a precarious existence in the cold. The Chesapeake has always provided valuable winter habitat to waterfowl—ducks, geese, and swans—that summer and breed farther north, in the Upper Midwest, Canada, and Alaska, but come here in winter to feed on underwater grasses and shellfish in generally ice-free waters.

A winter day on the Mattaponi near Bowling Green, Virginia, well above the influence of tide, shows low water with skim ice along the edges and ice coating the tree branches. DETAIL: *Storm clouds, from a 16th-century engraving.*

A sunset glows brightly in the clear winter air on the James River below Richmond. After the publication of Captain John Smith's map in 1612, eager colonists flocked to Virginia, but they settled this river first, from Jamestown all the way up to the falls, before spreading out onto the other Chesapeake waterways.

A stand of saltmarsh cordgrass, opposite, glows golden in autumn light along a marsh creek on the York River near Powhatan's capital of Werowocomoco. Though this plant offered little direct food value to the Indians, it has always played a key role in the high productivity of the Chesapeake's salt marshes.

Now began Smith's two-year association with the wily relatives, Opechancanough and Powhatan. He opened it by presenting the chief with a compass, which fascinated him. Even so, Opechancanough took the captain prisoner and marched him back to the lunch spot, where Smith found one of his crewmen killed by arrows and the other missing.

The natives took Smith on a long march from village to village on the Pamunkey and Mattaponi Rivers and even over to Toppahanock village, below today's Tappahannock on the Rappahannock, giving him a preliminary acquaintance with that river and motivating him to explore it the following summer. It turned out that the captain of a European ship had killed the chief of that town "the year before" (Smith's secondhand chronology was certainly inexact), and they wanted to know if he was the same person. "But the people reported him a great [tall] man that was captain" (whereas Smith was short).

Thus exonerated, he traveled south again to Powhatan's capital at Werowocomoco, on today's Purtan Bay on the York. In the process, Smith also got a look at today's Dragon Run, the headwaters of the Piankatank River, which he later also explored, at the end of the 1608 voyage.

Though Smith was frequently afraid for his life, Opechancanough's men treated him well and offered him more food than he could eat. During this odyssey and, indeed, all of his travels to date, Smith took pains to learn as much as he could of the Powhatan language. His soldier-of-fortune background had given him fluency in improvised sign language, but he also took pains to pick up the proper sounds of speech. He carried on extended conversations with Opechancanough about the compass and, beyond it, the Europeans' understanding of the nature of the Earth and its place in the universe. He also listened attentively to all that the natives told him about the geography of Virginia.

The meeting with Powhatan at Werowocomoco was a critical point in Jamestown's survival. Smith found the great chief in his longhouse, lying in splendor on an elevated bed, adorned with pearls and raccoon pelts, surrounded by his wives and his "chief men." There's no question that Powhatan was a very wise man. He sensed that the English presented unique and attractive trading opportunities in the short term, but that their perceived desire to settle the land and their superior technologies presented a grave long-term threat to his people's way of life.

Powhatan asked Smith the reason for the English settlement at Jamestown. Quick on his feet, Smith concocted a tale about being

swept into the Chesapeake by a storm and moving up the James to find fresh water, as well as to repair the ships. Powhatan countered with a question of why the colonists then explored upriver. Smith told him that they were looking for "the back sea" (the Pacific Ocean), and that natives had killed a child of Captain Newport's. They supposed the killers to have been Monacans, mortal enemies of Powhatan's people, who lived beyond the falls of the James. The English had tried to revenge the killing, without success so far.

Satisfied, Powhatan went on to describe the extent of his kingdom. Smith responded by describing Europe, ending with the statement that his "father" (chief, "king of all the waters") was Captain Newport, who would return from England soon. Powhatan asked Smith to leave Jamestown and move to the region of Werowocomoco, where the two groups would happily trade corn and venison for iron hatchets and

King Powhatan comands C: Smith to be slayne, his daughter Pokahontas beggs his life his thankfullne and how he subiected 39 of their kings, reade his history

led by James Reeue

copper goods. Smith promised to do so, and Powhatan sent him home with four escorts, plus a great deal of food.

At this point, there is an inconsistency between Smith's *True Relation* of 1608 and his longer *General History* of 1624. In the former, Powhatan sends Smith home without incident after their great conversation. The latter contains the celebrated story of Pocahontas throwing herself on Smith and begging her father to spare him as several warriors prepare to beat him to death. It may seem strange that Smith would at first have left out this event, or any mention of an attempt by Powhatan to have him executed. Pocahontas does, however, make a brief appearance at the end of the *True Relation,* in which he refers to her as being 10 years old. Hollywood aside, there appears to have been friendship between the native girl and the English adventurer but no romance.

DIPLOMACY AND SURVIVAL

*T*he day that Smith returned to Jamestown—January 2, 1608—Captain Newport arrived with additional colonists and provisions. A week later, the fort burned accidentally (no cause given), with loss of both life and belongings. As the colonists began to rebuild, Powhatan sent weekly presents of food, half for Smith and half for "his father" (Newport) "whom he much desired to see."

In February, the captains set forth to Werowocomoco by water, taking Smith around the corner at Point Comfort and up the Bayshore to the mouth of the York. This was full winter, and apparently a hard one full of ice, but Smith insisted on taking the Discovery Barge as a tender to the pinnace, *Discovery,* which Newport commanded for this trip.

The visit became a multiday "poker game" in which Smith and Powhatan maneuvered subtly to gain control, while being absolutely polite and kind to each other. There was clearly plenty of mutual respect in their relationship. Newport elected to stay aboard his ship the first day. Powhatan declared Smith a werowance of his kingdom (and therefore his subject), an honor that cut two ways, since it gave Smith great status among the natives around Jamestown but also meant that Powhatan expected him to seek permission before going off exploring.

The February weather was at first miserably wet, after which an apparent combination of clearing but strong northwest wind and a full

In this engraving, opposite, Pocahontas pleads for Smith's life, after her father, the paramount chief Powhatan, condemned him to death. The event may be legend, told by Smith in his General History *16 years later but not in his earlier journals.*

FOLLOWING PAGES: The Chesapeake Bay Foundation's education/ work boat Chesapeake *lies at a dock near Riverton, Maryland, on the Nanticoke River, with the mouth of Marshyhope Creek in the background. In the foreground, the strong growth and bright purple blooms of pickerelweed mark the time of year as late July or early August.*

or new moon caused an extremely low tide, which in turn caused great problems in moving around the shallow water at Werowocomoco. Smith, no stranger to hardship, marveled at the natives' capacity for cold, helping move the barge across frigid mud flats wearing only skimpy clothing, "though a dog would scarce have endured it."

On the second day, Newport came ashore, marched with Smith to Powhatan's house, and presented the great king with an English boy, 13-year-old Thomas Salvage (Savage), as a pledge of peace. The next day, Newport attempted to bargain with the chief for corn and, to Smith's consternation, gave away a dozen large copper cooking pots in exchange for "as much corn as at Chickahamania I had for one of less proportion."

After several more days of trading, feasting, dancing, and "mirth," Smith and Newport headed up the Pamunkey to visit Opechancanough and two of his brothers, Opitchapam and Kekataugh, at villages in the vicinity of today's Sweet Hall Landing. After several more days of trading and feasting, they returned to Werowocomoco, where Powhatan gave Newport one of his men, to go back to England as the captain's son, in exchange for Thomas Salvage. (Smith suspected that the chief wanted the man to "know our strength and the country's condition.") Then the barge and pinnace headed back to Jamestown with 250 bushels of corn.

In April, Newport weighed anchor to return to England, carrying turkeys sent by Powhatan in exchange for swords. Smith followed him down the river in the *Discovery Barge* and took a short trip up the Nansemond to trade, finding the people at first wary but then friendly, unlike the reception he would receive in early September, at the conclusion of his second trip up the bay. This time, he remarked on how attractive and productive the river's shores appeared to be.

Other trips up these two "working rivers" yielded more corn and continued jockeying for control with Powhatan and Opechancanough. One included an exploration up the Appomattox. In another, described in the opening quote during the winter of 1609, Smith and his crew took corn by force from Powhatan and Opechancanough while on an extended voyage up the York, Pamunkey, and Mattaponi that covered places he had visited on foot as a captive but now explored by water. He placed crosses up the Pamunkey at Hanovertown, near where Route 360 transverses the river today, and on the Mattaponi above today's village of Aylett.

The Mattaponi
and Pamunkey Rivers Today

*L*ike the Chickahominy, the Pamunkey and the Mattaponi drain bottomland swamps, and they remain even less settled than the Chickahominy. Though they have few cypresses, they still have the abundant freshwater marshes that fed Opechancanough's people 400 years ago, plus eagles and waterfowl. Descendants of Powhatan's people still fish for shad in both rivers each spring, operating from the Pamunkey and Mattaponi Indian Reservations, where both tribes operate shad hatcheries. American colonists settled much of the land along these two rivers

A whitetail doe looks out from the edge of a forest. Today, the "edge habitat" (cleared fields and house sites next to wooded areas) and the absence of natural predators have caused the whitetail deer population to explode in some parts of the watershed to levels beyond that of John Smith's time.

OPPOSITE PAGE:
Ferns grow in early spring on a patch of soil at the edge of Dragon Run, well upstream of its delta at the head of the Piankatank River. This long, wooded swamp does an effective job of filtering rainwater flowing to the river.

in the late 17th and 18th centuries, ruthlessly pushing the native people into their small reservations. It is a testimony to the pride of the people in the two surviving tribes, and to the value of their cultures, that they endure today, though they have had to adapt to the ways of modern society in the process.

The "metropolis" on the York is West Point, where the Pamunkey and the Mattaponi meet. From the 1870s until 1933, the town served as an important link where trains from Richmond met steamboats carrying freight and passengers to Baltimore. The town is best known, however, for the huge paper mill located at the mouth of the Pamunkey. The Clean Water Act has benefited the river considerably here.

The land downstream on the York is mostly rural, though the south bank is more built up because of its proximity to Williamsburg. On that side, military installations dominate the lower half of its 35-mile course. At Gloucester Point on the north side, the Virginia Institute of Marine Science, a division of the College of William and Mary, provides world-class research into the workings of the Chesapeake Bay ecosystem, while across the river lies historic Yorktown.

Today, the James and the York still serve us as working rivers, carrying naval ships, freighters, tugs with barges full of sand and gravel, and research vessels. Their utility, though, should not detract from their appeal. There is still enough of what John Smith saw in them to inspire us, and to make sure that we never take their health for granted.

INJURED, CAPTAIN SMITH RETURNS TO ENGLAND

*I*n September of 1609, Smith took the *Discovery Barge* to the falls of the James as part of a move to establish a satellite fort near there. On the way back, an accident injured him badly enough to send him back to England. One night, with the barge at anchor in mid-river, a spark ignited his gunpowder bag as he slept. Badly hurt, he jumped overboard to put out the resulting flames and would have drowned had his crew not pulled him back aboard. He left Virginia shortly thereafter, and though he eventually recovered from his injury, he never returned. Even so, he left a huge legacy for those who followed him.

Over the past four centuries, Captain John Smith has developed a reputation as the Chesapeake's first public relations consultant,

TUNDRA SWANS

 For many of us, swans are large, white birds with orange beaks that live year-round in parks. They are graceful to look at but bad tempered when approached up close. Those are mute swans, imports from Europe brought over as semidomesticated birds and supposedly kept in confinement.

Folks who visit the Chesapeake in winter know another species, tundra swans (formerly known as whistling swans). These birds spend the summer on Arctic tundra between Alaska's Bering Strait and Canada's Hudson Bay, breeding, nesting, and rearing their young (cygnets) to the point that they can make a 3,000-mile migration to the Chesapeake and the North Carolina sounds. The birds take their time doing so, spending three months from late August to mid-November working their way through the prairie pothole country of central Canada and the Dakotas before rolling in here just before Thanksgiving.

Some use the upper Chesapeake as a staging point for moving to areas farther south such as North Carolina's Lake Mattamuskeet, while others settle into areas with underwater grasses and soft-shell clams, from Maryland's Susquehanna Flats down into Virginia. There they while away the winter, often in the company of other waterfowl including American widgeon, which feed on material uprooted by the long-necked swans in depths that those ducks cannot reach.

On some rivers, the tundras mix occasionally with mute swans from the feral population that has grown on the bay after the escape of a group of cygnets from a pen in the 1960s. State waterfowl agencies in Maryland and Virginia are working to control the numbers of mutes, in part to protect the habitat of the tundras. Birds of a species that has been flying 3,000 miles one way for several thousand years to spend the winter here deserve a healthy habitat and the deep appreciation of the people who delight in watching them.

A tundra swan prepares to take off from a cove on the lower York River on a snowy day. In recent years, the birds have had to search hard to find the underwater grass beds that they prefer for food.
DETAIL: *A tundra swan, from a 16th-century engraving.*

a shameless promoter for the Virginia Company who hedged the truth. Fanciful movie depictions of his nonexistent romance with Pocahontas have added a cartoonish quality to that reputation. But a friend who recently circumnavigated the Delmarva Peninsula in a kayak, visiting the sites of a number of Smith's explorations, declared him "a hell of a man or a hell of a liar."

The statement was one of respect. This friend has read Smith's journals and studied the 1612 map. The details in them must form the foundation for any modern evaluation of Smith's character. The map, especially, is uncannily accurate in the waters he mapped, given the tools he had to work with at the time. He really did go everywhere he said he did.

Smith's *True Relation* had already been published, without his knowledge, in London in 1608. The publisher derived it from the report Smith sent back in June of that year while aboard the *Phoenix,* just before his first exploration up the Chesapeake in the *Discovery Barge.*

John Smith's map was published in Oxford, England, in 1612, accompanied by *The Description of Virginia,* which includes Smith's classic description of the Chesapeake quoted here in Chapter One. Widely distributed and often copied, the map served as the blueprint for settlement of the Chesapeake and its rivers for the remainder of the 17th century. Consider for a moment the degree to which that settlement established a cornerstone for what would become the United States. As Smith scholar Edward Wright Haile has declared, "If George Washington [a son of two rivers that Smith explored] is the father of our country, John Smith is the grandfather."

Over the next 20 years, the English spread out to establish plantations along the James and York Rivers. After John Rolfe, husband-to-be of Powhatan's favored daughter, Pocahontas, raised the first commercially profitable crop of tobacco at Varina Plantation on the James, the driving economic force became growing and shipping large quantities of the now-fashionable weed to England.

Meanwhile, John Smith met Captain William Claiborne in London around 1620, showed him the map, and persuaded him to throw in his lot with the Virginia Colony. Claiborne arrived in 1621, served as the secretary of the colony, and at the request of the governor, began to explore again the upper Chesapeake, including the three Eastern Shore rivers that Smith missed: the Choptank, the Eastern Bay system, and the Chester. In 1631, he established a trading post for the

local Indians on Kent Island, with satellite operations on Poplar, Sharp's, and Palmer's Islands, the latter lying in the mouth of the Susquehanna and now named Garrett Island. Ed Haile believes that Captain Smith knew Garrett Island because he had met the Susquehannocks on the Discovery Barge's second voyage in the summer of 1608 and told Claiborne that it was a natural trading place.

Lord Baltimore's colonists used the map to establish the Maryland colony at St. Mary's City on the lower Potomac in 1634. (They later claimed Kent and Garrett Islands for Maryland and drove Claiborne's people away.) And John Washington, great-grandfather of Gen. George Washington, used Smith's map to settle on the Virginia side of the Potomac at Popes Creek in 1654, at the site where the general would be born in 1732.

In 1673, Augustine Herrman published his updated map, which filled in the few blanks on Smith's 1612 effort and noted counties (already established) and settlements as well as some navigation information. Throughout the next hundred years leading up to the American Revolution, a strong and cultured plantation society grew up around the bay and its tributaries.

What made Captain John Smith so enthusiastic about the Chesapeake? Despite the fact that he did not find the two quick-riches resources the Virginia Company's stockholders most desired—precious metals and a "Northwest Passage" to China—he sensed the economic potential of the region for people like himself with a strong work ethic. Thanks to his explorations, he had a comprehensive sense of the infrastructure of navigable rivers that the region offered to a decentralized economy based on agriculture and timber.

For the next 200 years, that vision played out both in Maryland and in Virginia, with the one major shift being a move by some plantation owners, especially George Washington, from tobacco to more diversified crops. Meanwhile, the tidal rivers also opened up the inner lands of the two colonies, with ports of entry growing at their fall lines. Thus Richmond sprang up on the James (at the site that Smith described as Powhatan), Fredericksburg on the Rappahannock, Alexandria and Georgetown on the Potomac, Elkridge on the Patapsco, and Havre de Grace and Port Deposit on the Susquehanna. Meanwhile, the English also moved into the Eastern Shore rivers, including the Chester, Wye, Miles, and Choptank, which Smith had missed.

Even then Smith's "faire Bay" was still "compassed but for the mouth with fruitful and delightsome land." In those 200 years, the English had become Americans, Virginia and Maryland had become two of the 13 original United States, slavery of Africans had become entrenched, and the native tribes had become almost totally dispersed or absorbed into the new culture. Meanwhile, the newcomers had introduced horses, machinery, and metal tools, but the culture still ran on muscle, wind, or water power. Though Richmond had begun to grow up on the hills around the falls of the James, Chief Powhatan's son Tanxpowhatan would still have recognized the surroundings of his old village.

The early 19th century, however, brought great upheaval. Deep plows cleaved the fields on the coastal plain and the Piedmont, sending millions of tons of soil downstream. The discovery of steam power unlocked the stored fossil energy in coal, to power a new invention, the railroad, and expand manufacturing in the region's growing cities, though much of its rural landscape remained agricultural. The growth of the nation's capital at Washington, D.C., required great quantities of wood (for construction lumber and fuel), sand and gravel (for concrete and roadways), and food (both farm produce and seafood).

After the Civil War, manufacturing grew even more, and steam power greatly expanded our capability to harvest bay resources. Meanwhile, cities such as Richmond, Washington, and Salisbury, Maryland, built "combined sewer systems" designed to carry both stormwater and household sewage in the same underground pipes that ran to "primary treatment" plants, which allowed solids to

The fluffy feathers on newborn great blue herons, opposite, look soft, but their heavy, powerful bills hint strongly at the fishing prowess the chicks will soon acquire. These birds were hatched at Watts Island, a remote rookery five miles east-southeast of Tangier Island, Virginia, that belongs to the U.S. Fish and Wildlife Service and is managed by staff from the Blackwater National Wildlife Refuge.

settle out before discharge of the wastewater to the rivers. In dry weather there was no problem, but even moderate rainstorms caused the systems to overflow through storm drains, sending raw sewage overboard in large quantities. The combined systems doubtless seemed like good ideas at the time, with the economy of building only one set of pipes, and this primitive treatment system greatly reduced disease in the cities—for people who never came into contact with the rivers. Meanwhile, petroleum unlocked even greater fossil-derived energy with the advent of the internal combustion engine and the electric power plant.

The region's population grew explosively through the 20th century. By Jamestown's 350th anniversary in 1957, the combination of sewage, roadways, rooftops, intensive agriculture, and electric power around the Chesapeake had seriously fouled the bay's air and water. Public health officials in urban centers like Norfolk/Portsmouth, Richmond, Washington, and Baltimore advised strongly against direct contact with the adjacent waters. The wonderful character of the Chesapeake and the successors to Smith's map had drawn us humans here with tools and in numbers that Captain John Smith could never have foreseen.

Fortunately, the people of the Chesapeake region awoke to the damage to the bay's ecosystem beginning with the passage of the Clean Water Act, and the restoration movement has continued, especially since the first interjurisdictional Chesapeake Bay Agreement was signed in 1983. Today, we have made modest progress, but we struggle always against the heavy footprint of human population growth, currently bringing in a million new people each decade. As this book goes to press in the spring of 2006, the population of the Chesapeake Bay watershed is 16 million, approximately twice what it was at Jamestown's 350th anniversary.

If he returned today, Captain John Smith would be amazed but no doubt also appalled by the changes. In 1607-09, his overwhelming and immediate concerns were personal and collective survival in a vast and frequently unfriendly land, but he clearly loved this natural treasure. Today, he'd be pleased with our modest progress at restoration, but he would urge us forward, challenge us to love the Chesapeake well: to explore it, know firsthand all of its riches, restore its health, and teach our children to act as good stewards of its future. Surely, it—and we—deserve no less.

A brilliant sunset closes another day on the Chesapeake. Though the great pressure of human population will never again allow the bay to return to the pristine condition that Captain John Smith and his crew saw, there is reason to hope that the people of the region are reawakening to a new appreciation of this national treasure in their midst and rededicating themselves to restoring its health.

Exploring the Chesapeake by Boat

*I*n 1971, the Chesapeake Bay Foundation's executive director, Arthur Sherwood, based the foundation's education program on a simple idea: "The place to teach people about the bay is on it and in it." Today, that field-trip program serves 40,000 students, teachers, and other adults each year, a testament to the power of Sherwood's vision. Anyone who seeks to understand the significance of Captain John Smith's explorations of the Chesapeake would do well to heed Arthur Sherwood's advice and get out on the historic water trail. Firsthand experience is the surest way to learn why Smith was so excited about the Chesapeake and to see why it remains a national treasure today.

"But I'm an experienced boatman," you may say. "I already know it." Ask yourself, do you really know it the way Smith came to know it, in all seasons, up the big rivers to the head of navigation as well as up the main stem? Only a very few enterprising cruising sailors, trawler skippers, kayak paddlers, and other boaters have covered as much of the bay in their lifetimes as John Smith did in two and a half years. That's too bad. The Chesapeake is large—far and away the most extensive estuary on the North American continent—but it is approachable because its unique network of rivers reaches deep into the lands around it and, thus, into people's lives. There is still much that every one of us can learn from it, whether we try to explore the whole water trail or cover just one river carefully. There are satisfying surprises there for anyone who looks.

Because of its riverine structure, the bay is remarkably varied, especially moving from fresh to brackish and salty water, so there is plenty to learn about how all of its parts fit together ecologically. That understanding, which begins to come quickly with time on the water, is the key to understanding its ecological richness, even today with the heavy footprint of 16 million 21st-century people holding it down to one-quarter of its potential productivity.

All of that ecological variation has produced a rich fabric of regional human cultures, beginning with Native Americans and leading through four centuries to today. Many books document these cultures, but what brings them to life is actually to visit them. The relationships between the Chesapeake and its people range from local, regional, and international transport to multifaceted seafood harvesting and recreation. The bay and its rivers have literally wound their way through our lives. Together, they form the dominant natural resources for our region.

CHOOSING A VESSEL

The bay and its rivers fit a wide range of boats for those who would explore them on their own. For modern-day explorers who do not own their own vessels or who are less confident of their water skills, there is a wide range of other options—from rentals and charters to guided tours and, in some places, large, comfortable tour boats. Virtually any sound watercraft can cover some parts of the trail well. What I offer here are my personal opinions, but thanks to my father, Arthur Sherwood, and various friends, I am fortunate to base them on 63 years of experience that has covered virtually the whole trail in a variety of vessels.

SELF-PROPELLED PADDLING AND ROWING BOATS are fundamental in getting to know the Chesapeake well. The gentle, two-to-six miles-per-hour speed and the rhythm of paddling and rowing, close to the water, lend them to absorbing the sense of a creek or river. I have no doubt that Smith took in a lot of the details that went into his map while taking his turn at the *Discovery Barge*'s oars and tiller, and he certainly worked on his notebook while his crew was rowing.

Modern sea kayaks have become vessels of choice for many Chesapeake explorers. They are quick, durable, seaworthy, and relatively inexpensive boats, among the few classes of vessel capable of covering the entire John Smith water trail. While only the most experienced and well-conditioned paddlers should attempt the trail's large open-water passages, most paddlers who have learned safe kayaking practices can explore many of the trail's most interesting upriver and along-shore sections. Some kayak outfitters are now gearing up to give novice paddlers opportunities to explore parts of the trail with experienced field guides.

Canoes move more slowly and cannot take the seas that kayaks with spray skirts can handle, but they tend to be more stable and carry larger loads (including families), making them ideal for shorter trips. Much of my own coverage of the trail's rivers came while leading Chesapeake Bay Foundation field trips with a fleet of nine 17-foot Grumman canoes in the 1970s and 1980s. Like family vans and pickup trucks, canoes still have plenty of uses around the Chesapeake.

The great advantage of both classes of paddle craft is the huge range of access they offer. In addition to conventional launch ramps, many road crossings offer adequate, safe launching areas. At present, much of the shoreline along the water trail is privately owned, so setting up an agenda for a multiday expedition with nightly campsites is difficult. It is very easy to string together a succession of day trips with overnights at commercial campgrounds, B&B's, or motels, but true camp-along-the-river experience is still difficult to get. One hope for the water trail is that it will lead to at least a few more legitimate waterfront campsites.

Serious rowing boats still represent a small (though enthusiastic and skillful) subculture among self-propelled boaters. Whitehalls, wherries, peapods, Adirondack guide boats, recreational shells, and similar vessels make great boats for exploration, too, especially on rivers where powerful oars provide good antidotes to strong currents. Rowing boats, however, generally weigh more than canoes and kayaks and, as such, require more finished launching facilities. But there's nothing quite like a vigorous row down a beautiful river.

TRAILERED SAILBOATS AND POWERBOATS form another useful class, because they can take advantage of the large number of launch ramps around the water trail. Sailors should note that currents from the combination of tidal and downstream flow become quite strong in the upper sections of the trail's rivers. Another problem is beating into the wind in narrow, meandering channels. (Remember the *Discovery Barge*'s trials on the James and other rivers.) In many cases, creative use of launch points will help avoid problems with masts and bridges. Sailing a small vessel, especially one equipped with oars, is arguably the purest way to emulate Captain John Smith's experience. It is not, however, the easiest.

After ten years of short day trips in the Chesapeake Bay Foundation's canoe fleet, I developed great curiosity about how the parts of the bay's rivers fitted together. Starting in 1988, I began prowling them with a group of friends in 16- to 20-foot outboard-powered skiffs. It was an eye-opening experience to "unroll these rivers" at 20 miles per hour instead of canoe speed, in some cases tying together as many as a dozen areas where I had run school field trips or fished with my father as a boy.

These boats, most of them seaworthy but shallow-draft center console skiffs, have proven to be great river vehicles, capable of handling nasty weather but still able to sneak into tiny creeks, especially if equipped with proper pushpoles. There have been times, too, when I was glad to be traveling in a pair of sturdy hip boots, which allowed

CHESAPEAKE

me to get out and tow my 17-foot skiff like a canal boat mule. Combining short, intense explorations by self-propelled craft with longer trips in capable small powerboats is an excellent way to see much—if not all—of the Captain John Smith Water Trail.

As with canoes and kayaks, running small powerboats on these waters takes prudence and carefully won experience, as well as thoughtful choice of rig and common courtesy. Running an internal combustion engine on a water trail carries with it serious responsibility. Modern "clean" four-stroke and direct-injected two-stroke outboards are certainly the best choices for these explorations. Not only do they eliminate the blue smoke of old-style two-stroke engines, but they are much quieter and more fuel-efficient, especially at the low speeds appropriate for prowling up small tributaries.

It's easy to rig one with a GPS chartplotter and a fishfinder, especially in a compact combination unit. Both can teach a great deal about the rivers. If equipped with a chart card, the plotter is a valuable aid to following a regional water trail map like the one developed for Smith's travels on the James River by Virginia's Department of Conservation and Recreation, or the one for the Nanticoke River trail from the Maryland Department of Natural Resources. Meanwhile, the fishfinder will show the extraordinary channels the Chesapeake's rivers carve in their beds as well as the way they move sand, gravel, and mud around—and, of course, the fish living in them. You'll learn a lot about why places such as Leedstown on the Rappahannock and Georgetown on the Sassafras have been village sites since the 1500s.

A waterman from Smith Island, Maryland, opposite, pulls a "hand scrape" (toothless dredge) through eelgrass beds to catch peeler and soft crabs. Boats like his are built to run in very shallow water on the flats around Tangier Sound.

LARGER CRUISING SAILBOATS AND POWERBOATS are the most comfortable vessels of all for covering the open-water passages and broad harbors of the trail. Sailing brings awareness of the factors that Smith had to deal with, especially wind and current, and approximates his pace of travel. Kent Mountford, an accomplished sailor and veteran Chesapeake marine scientist, has sailed many of Smith's specific open-water routes with the express purpose of studying the conditions under which the *Discovery Barge* traveled. His observations appear in the excellent new book *John Smith's Chesapeake Voyages, 1607-1609.*

As with small sailboats, larger cruising boats must deal with the difficult winds on the Chesapeake rivers' narrow channels and meander bends. They must also deal with bridges and a general lack of marina services, including readily-accessible fuel and shore-power hookups. Trawlers generally fit the water trail's requirements well because of their fuel efficiency, self-sufficiency, and unobtrusive wakes, though those with flying bridges must also deal with limited-clearance bridges.

In another class are the single-engine, 28- to 45-foot sedan or express power cruisers based on working hulls from New England and the Chesapeake. These boats are also self-sufficient and move well at both slow (6-9 mph) and moderate (14-22 mph) speeds. As with new outboards, the advent of new clean, quiet diesels adds much to the attractiveness of these boats as water trail cruisers. The fact that keels with skegs protect their single propellers from obstructions is an additional advantage.

Commercial tour boats offer attractive alternatives for people who want their explorations ready-made. The elevated deck of a sight-seeing vessel is a good vantage point for absorbing the sweep of a harbor, and traveling this way recaptures the joys of one of the Chesapeake eras that followed Smith's explorations, that of the river steamboats of 1865-1933.

The Great Chesapeake Paradox

As you explore the bay and its rivers, you may wonder, on a heavily impacted river like the Anacostia, "What is the use of even trying to clean it up?" or on a great beauty like the Nanticoke at its confluence with Marshyhope Creek, "What's the problem?"

The catch is that they are two elements of the same reality. The Chesapeake is big, and it challenges us to be big, too—big in exploring it, big in understanding it, and big in caring for its future. In seeing both its best and its worst, we must remember the huge ecological richness that John Smith and his crews saw, and understand that we can still unlock some of that potential with careful and patient, but vigorous and persistent, restoration. One more time: We owe no less to the Chesapeake, ourselves, and our children.

For anyone who travels Captain John Smith's water trail, it is important to remember two primary issues: safety and common courtesy. The former means fitting one's boating skills and choice of vessel to a particular waterway and set of weather conditions. The second means respecting the safety and needs of other boaters, their vessels, and the waterways, including shorelines. A power cruiser up the James has no right to threaten kayaks with its wake, but neither do those kayaks have the right to obstruct a tug pushing a tow of gravel barges. Exploring the water trail is, after all, about fitting in with and absorbing the ways of the Chesapeake and its people, not mistreating them.

A faithful friend enjoys the breeze on the bow of a johnboat as her master explores a marsh creek near Tangier Sound's Cedar Strait, through which Captain John Smith brought the Discovery Barge *after visiting the Wighcocomoco (Pocomoke) River. On the south side of Cedar Strait is the Chesapeake Bay Foundation's education center on Great Fox Island.*

Further Reading

Books

Three Essentials

Haile, Edward Wright, ed. *Jamestown Narratives: Eyewitness Accounts of the Virginia Colony, The First Decade: 1607-1617*. Champlain, VA: RoundHouse, 1998. This exhaustive collection of primary sources for Jamestown and John Smith's explorations, including *A True Relation, A Map of Virginia,* and *The General History,* includes valuable commentary by Smith scholar Edward Wright Haile.

Price, David A. *Love and Hate in Jamestown: John Smith, Pocahontas, and the Heart of a New Nation*. New York: Alfred A. Knopf, 2003. An excellent, well-researched narrative history of Jamestown from the colonists' departure from England through the critical first 15 years of the colony, with an excellent concluding chapter, "Smith's Vision for America."

Rountree, Helen C., et al. *John Smith's Chesapeake Voyages, 1607-1609*. Charlottesville, VA: University of Virginia Press, 2006. A comprehensive account of the Chesapeake ecosystem in 1607, the cultures of the natives and the English, and the history of John Smith's voyages, written by an interdisciplinary team of historians, sociologists, archaeologists, and marine scientists.

Useful Background

Gleach, Frederic W. *Powhatan's World in Colonial Virginia: A Conflict of Cultures*. Lincoln, NE: University of Nebraska Press, 1997. An authoritative examination of the Algonquian cultures of the Chesapeake in the 17th century.

LeGrand, Martha, ed. *Guide to Cruising the Chesapeake Bay*. Annapolis, MD: *Chesapeake Bay Magazine*, 2007. A big-boat cruising guide published annually by *Chesapeake Bay Magazine* that concentrates primarily on marina facilities and navigation information.

Rountree, Helen C., and Thomas E. Davidson. *Eastern Shore Indians of Virginia and Maryland*. Charlottesville, VA: University of Virginia Press, 1997. An artful blend of sociology and ecology.

Rountree, Helen C. *Pocahontas, Powhatan, Opechancanough: Three Indian Lives Changed by Jamestown.* Charlottesville, VA: University of Virginia Press, 2005. A thoughtful discussion of 17th-century Virginia from the point of view of the natives.

Schmidt, Susan. *Landfall along the Chesapeake: In the Wake of Captain John Smith.* Baltimore, MD: Johns Hopkins University Press, 2006. A lively account of a voyage that covered much of Captain John Smith's routes, taken in the summer and fall of 2002 by a marine scientist and English professor with her dog.

Shellenberger, William H. *Cruising the Chesapeake: A Gunkholer's Guide.* Camden, ME: International Marine Publishing, 1990. A big-boat cruiser's guide that covers open-water sections of the bay well and includes good information for exploring by dinghy.

Williams, John Page. *Exploring the Chesapeake in Small Boats.* Centreville, MD: Tidewater Publishers, 1992. This is a book I wrote specifically for people in canoes, kayaks, and outboard skiffs to help them explore the Chesapeake's upper tidal rivers, for which no other bay-wide cruise guide exists. It includes information about the ecology of Chesapeake rivers through the seasons of the year as well as information on using specific kinds of boats.

MAPS

ADC's Waterproof Chartbook of the Chesapeake Bay (*www.adcmap.com*). A large-format, spiral-bound, waterproof navigational chart book of the entire Chesapeake Bay and its tributaries, including a listing of launch ramps and marina facilities. Excellent for general reference and small boat navigation.

Chesapeake Bay & Susquehanna River Public Access Guide, EPA Chesapeake Bay Program (*www.chesapeakebay.net*). A free and useful map of access points around the Chesapeake.

Haile, Edward Wright. *England in America: The Chesapeake Bay from Jamestown to St. Mary's City, 1607-1634.* Champlain, VA: RoundHouse, 1999. Settlement patterns resulting from Captain John Smith's 1612 map.

Haile, Edward Wright. *Virginia Discovered & Described by Captayn John Smith, 1608.* Champlain, VA: RoundHouse, 1999. A readable version of Smith's map, including the sites of native villages.

John Smith's Adventures on the James River. Richmond: Virginia Department of Conservation and Recreation, 2005.

PAGE 184:
The author holds his canoe on the edge of a cattail marsh on the Patuxent River just below Jug Bay and just upriver of the 17th century site of the werowance village of Mattapanient. Captain John Smith placed his Patuxent River cross a half-mile south of here.

Websites

National Geographic Society, *www.nationalgeographic.com/chesapeake*. Includes interactive maps, video, travel guides, links to National Geographic articles and classroom materials.

Captain John Smith 400, *www.johnsmith400.org*. Information about the 400th anniversary including a chart of the Chesapeake, itineraries for the *Discovery Barge*'s 2006 museum tour and 2007 voyage reenactment, and social studies curriculum for middle schools.

Chesapeake Gateways Network, *www.baygateways.net*. Visitor information for more than 130 of the Chesapeake Bay's hidden treasures, including parks, wildlife refuges, maritime museums, historic sites, Indian reservations, and water trails.

Historic Jamestown, *www.nps.gov/colo/Jamestwn/jamestown.htm*. Descriptions of National Park Service facilities on Jamestown Island, including guided tours.

Jamestown 1607 (VA Tourism Corporation), *www.jamestown1607.org*. Information about *The New World* film, stories of the voyage from England, and an interactive game.

Jamestown 2007, *jamestown2007.org*. A detailed listing of upcoming events in 2006 and 2007 relating to the 400th anniversary.

Jamestown Rediscovery (Association for the Preservation of Virginia Antiquities), *www.apva.org/jr.html*. Notes on the archaeology and history of the Jamestown fort.

Jamestown Settlement (Jamestown-Yorktown Foundation), *www.history isfun.org/historyisfun.org*. Information about upcoming special programs and extensive new exhibits, including the three recreated ships, as well as information for reenactors.

Maryland Department of Natural Resources, *dnr.state.md.us*. Potomac, Patuxent, and Nanticoke water trail maps.

Mattaponi/Pamunkey Water Trail Map (Mattaponi-Pamunkey Rivers Association), *www.mpra.org*. Excellent trail maps for purchase.

Virginia Department of Conservation and Recreation, *www.johnsmith trail.org*. Information on the James River Water Trail, including driving tours and printable maps.

Virginia's Indians, Past & Present, *falcon.jmu.edu/~ramseyil/vaindians.htm*. Historical and current information about Virginia's Indian tribes.

Virtual Jamestown (Virginia Center for Digital History), *www.virtual jamestown.org*. A dynamic digital map of the Jamestown settlement with many interactive features.

ACKNOWLEDGMENTS

Many people have helped me return to the 17th century in this quest for Captain John Smith and the Chesapeake he saw. The first is Patrick F. Noonan, chairman emeritus of The Conservation Fund, whose vision and enthusiasm for the Captain John Smith Chesapeake National Historic Water Trail has inspired many people, organizations, and government agencies. He has been a valuable advisor and mentor to me throughout this project. Also from The Conservation Fund, Nancy Merrill and Joel Dunn have been invaluable colleagues.

Many Chesapeake Bay Foundation staff members are involved in the John Smith Water Trail as well as in restoring the Chesapeake. They especially include President Will Baker, Vice Presidents Roy Hoagland and Don Baugh, web guru Kim Ethridge, and master educator/naturalist Bill Portlock, also a major photographer for this book. Many staff at the National Geographic Society are involved with Captain Smith and the Water Trail. For this project, they include Chairman Gil Grosvenor; his deputy, Bob Dulli; Barbara Brownell Grogan from the Book Division; and the project's editor, Garrett Brown, and his talented team. I have learned a lot about book-making from them. Also due for thanks are the three superb photographers whose images grace this book—Anthony E. Cook, Dave Harp, and Bill Portlock.

Other folks from whom I have learned a great deal include Edward Wright Haile and Deanna Beacham. Ed is the creator of the extraordinary volume *Jamestown Narratives: Eyewitness Accounts of the Virginia Colony, The First Decade, 1607-1617*. This 946-page labor of love was sparked in part by his living all his life across the Rappahannock River from Fones Cliffs, where Captain Smith and his crew repulsed an attack from Rapahannock warriors. Ed has been both an advisor and a companion on various segments of the Water Trail. Deanna is program specialist for the Virginia Council on Indians. She has worked tirelessly to make sure that the native peoples' point of view is woven fairly into all stories told about Captain Smith and the Jamestown Colony.

Regional water trails will add depth to this National Historic Water Trail. As of this writing, John Davy and his staff at Virginia's Department of Conservation and Recreation have unveiled a wonderful Smith-related trail for the James River and are working on more. Likewise, Lisa Gutierrez and her staff at Maryland's Department of Natural Resources are working on a Nanticoke River Trail, with more to come. Meanwhile, Bill Street, a former CBF colleague and now executive director of the James River Association, is working on a map of the James's wonderful tributary, the Chickahominy, with Steve Adkins, current chief of the Chickahominy Tribe.

Finally, I must thank my colleagues at the Chesapeake Bay Foundation for bearing with my considerable absences during the writing of this book and my wife, Louise, whose busy life I continually disrupted in the execution of that task.

The Book Division wishes to thank Pat Noonan for his inspiration and guidance throughout the project. We also thank historian John Davenport of Mosquito Point, Virginia, and Bob and Cherri Marvin of Charlottesville and *Rivanna* on the Chesapeake for help in conceptualizing this book.

ABOUT THE AUTHOR

John Page Williams grew up in Richmond, Virginia, and on the lower Potomac River, near Kinsale, Virginia. As a boy, he fished and explored many of the waters of the Captain John Smith Water Trail with his father. He has been a member of the Chesapeake Bay Foundation staff since 1973, serving as a field educator, program administrator, fundraiser, and staff writer while running field trips by canoe, outboard skiff, and workboat on every river system in the Chesapeake.

In his current position as senior naturalist, he serves as the lead CBF staffer in the partnership with The Conservation Fund and the National Geographic Society to develop the Captain John Smith Chesapeake National Historic Water Trail. He also works on a grassroots campaign to develop a strong, active constituency of anglers and boaters throughout the Chesapeake-Susquehanna watershed participating in programs to improve water quality and restore the ecosystem's health. In his spare time, Williams reviews boats and marine electronics and writes on fishing and environmental issues for *Boating, Chesapeake Bay,* and *Offshore* magazines.

ILLUSTRATION CREDITS

CHESAPEAKE

EXPLORING THE WATER TRAIL OF CAPTAIN JOHN SMITH

JOHN PAGE WILLIAMS

Published by the National Geographic Society

John M. Fahey, Jr., President and Chief Executive Officer

Gilbert M. Grosvenor, Chairman of the Board

Nina D. Hoffman, Executive Vice President;
    President, Books Publishing Group

Prepared by the Book Division

Kevin Mulroy, Senior Vice President and Publisher

Leah Bendavid-Val, Director of Photography Publishing
    and Illustrations

Marianne R. Koszorus, Director of Design

Barbara Brownell Grogan, Executive Editor

Elizabeth Newhouse, Director of Travel Publishing

Carl Mehler, Director of Maps

Staff for This Book

Garrett Brown, Editor

Judith Klein, Developmental Editor

John Thompson, Contributing Editor

Kate Griffin, Illustrations Editor

Suzanne Crawford, Copy Editor

Cinda Rose, Art Director

Sanaa Akkach, Designer

Steven D. Gardner, Lisa R. Ritter, and NG Maps, Map Research
    and Production

Teresa Tate, Illustrations Specialist

Lewis Bassford, Production Project Manager

Rebecca Hinds, Managing Editor

Gary Colbert, Production Director

Manufacturing and Quality Management

Christopher A. Liedel, Chief Financial Officer

Phillip L. Schlosser, Vice President

John T. Dunn, Technical Director

Vincent P. Ryan, Director

Chris Brown, Director

Maryclare Tracy, Manager

Printed in the United States of America.

Founded in 1888, the National Geographic Society is
one of the largest nonprofit scientific and educational
organizations in the world. It reaches more than 285
million people worldwide each month through its
official journal, NATIONAL GEOGRAPHIC, and its four
other magazines; the National Geographic Channel;
television documentaries; radio programs; films;
books; videos and DVDs; maps; and interactive
media. National Geographic has funded more than
8,000 scientific research projects and supports an
education program combating geographic illiteracy.

For more information, please call
1-800-NGS LINE (647-5463)
or write to the following address:

National Geographic Society
1145 17th Street N.W.
Washington, D.C. 20036-4688 U.S.A.

Visit us online at www.nationalgeographic.com

For information about special discounts for bulk purchases,
please contact National Geographic Books Special Sales:
ngspecsales@ngs.org

Deluxe Edition (2006)
ISBN-10: 0-7922-5557-7
ISBN-13: 978-0-7922-5557-4

Cloth Special Publication (2006)
ISBN-10: 0-7922-5556-9
ISBN-13: 978-0-7922-5556-7

Trade Softcover (2007)
ISBN-10: 1-4262-0069-2
ISBN-13: 978-1-4262-0069-4

Library of Congress Cataloging-in-Publication Data

Williams, John Page, 1942-
  Chesapeake : exploring the water trail of Captain John
Smith / by John Page Williams ; foreword by Gil Grosvenor.
    p. cm.
  Includes index.
  ISBN-13: 978-0-7922-5556-7 (cloth : alk. paper)
  ISBN-13: 978-0-7922-5557-4 (deluxe : alk. paper)
  ISBN-13: 978-1-4262-0069-4 (pbk. : alk. paper)
  1. Smith, John, 1580-1631--Travel--Chesapeake Bay (Md.
and Va.) 2. Chesapeake Bay (Md. and Va.)--Description and
travel. 3. Chesapeake Bay (Md. and Va.)--History--Pictorial
works. 4. Chesapeake Bay (Md. and Va.)--Pictorial works. 5.
Chesapeake Bay (Md. and Va.)--Guidebooks. 6. Boats and
boating--Chesapeake Bay (Md. and Va.)--Guidebooks. 7.
Water trails--Chesapeake Bay (Md. and Va.)--Guidebooks.
I. Title.
  F187.C5W46 2006
  551.46'1347--dc22
                                    2006015736